Some Assembly Required:

A Networking Guide for Graduates

by Anne Brown and Thom Singer

New Year Publishing, LLC
Danville, California

Some Assembly Required:
A Networking Guide for Graduates

by Thom Singer & Anne Brown
Copyright © 2010

Published by:
New Year Publishing, LLC
144 Diablo Ranch Ct.
Danville, CA 94506 USA
http://www.newyearpublishing.com

ISBN 978-1-9355470-8-2 (Paperback)
ISBN 978-1-9355471-4-3 (Hardcover)
Library of Congress Control Number:

Printed in the U.S.A.

This book is dedicated to my late father, Joe Brockseker, who never networked a day in his life, but made friends everywhere he went.

–Anne Brown

This book is dedicated to my wife, Sara, and my daughters, Jackie and Kate. You are as much a part of this project as anyone in the way you support my writing and speaking career. Thank you!

–Thom Singer

ACKNOWLEDGEMENTS

This book would not have been possible without the encouragement and support of some amazing people. First, thank you Dave Morris and Thom Singer for giving me the opportunity to work with you. It's been a pleasure.

To my husband Aaron, thank you for an endless supply of encouragement and humor. You never cease to make me laugh out loud. To Hannah, I'm sorry there aren't any pictures of cows in this one, baby. Thanks to my mom and sister for the morning coffee ichats. Thank you Carmen Brown for becoming Southwest Airlines' best customer so that Hannah wouldn't get lonely when I had to work.

And a very special thank you to Karyn McCoy for coming on board to help me run my business and life while completing this project.

–Anne Brown

I would like to thank Anne Brown for her outstanding dedication to this book. It is the fourth book in the *Some Assembly Required* series and one that I know will touch the lives of countless graduates looking to make the leap into their careers. Also, it could not have been possible without Marny Lifshen (co-author of *Some Assembly Required: A Networking Guide for Women*) and Chad Goldwasser (co-author of *Some Assembly Required: A Networking Guide for Real Estate*).

Special appreciation goes to my father-in-law, Bob Phelan, for proof-reading the final draft of the book. His lifetime career as a language teacher has made him a valuable part of my writing team!

As always, special thanks goes to Dave and Leslie Morris, who are both my friends and business partners. You continue to lead by example in the way you support all the people in your lives. This book could never have happened without your vision.

–Thom Singer

CONTENTS

INTRODUCTION

There are many misperceptions among college graduates about the value of networking. They range from "networking is a waste of time" to "networking is only for people in sales and real estate" to "no one is interested in hearing what I have to say at networking events so why bother?" Though it's no mystery why graduates are feeling discouraged these days, don't take it out on networking. It hasn't done anything to you, but it *can* do so much *for* you. In fact, in today's economy, building a network of business contacts is *the most important thing* you can do to give your career the booster shot it needs to thrive.

Here's why:

You already have the knowledge and skills; all you need now is a chance to prove yourself. Whether you want to work for a large corporation, a non-profit, start your own business, or do all three, it's the people who know, like, and trust you who will ultimately present you with that chance. That's because these are the people who will turn you on to job openings, recommend you for those résumés-building positions, and simply be there to offer words of wisdom when you need them most, even if you don't always want to hear them.

There are also many misconceptions about networking. Some recent graduates expect that it will be easy to make friends in business because they were such social butterflies at school. They assume networking relationships just happen naturally; *why spend time learning how to network?* Others point to luck or family connections as being automatic paths that lead to professional wins. The reality is: building a successful network does not happen by accident, nor can it be done for you. No matter who you are, where you're from, or what college you attended, building a successful network takes work, time, intent, and the willingness to help others. However, we promise that if you use this book as a guide, you will learn how to form a professional and personal network all your own, one that will have a profound impact on your life and career.

Some Assembly Required: A Networking Guide for Graduates is the eighth book from award-winning speaker Thom Singer, and the fourth book in his "Some Assembly Required" series. His co-author of this book, Anne Brown, is the founder of the popular website *GradtoGreat.com* for college graduates making the transition from college to career. Like Thom's other books, this book is based on the premise that people prefer to hire and do business with those they know, like, and trust.

The strategies presented in these pages may seem deceptively simple. However, once you incorporate them into your routine, you'll be amazed at how much easier achieving your dreams becomes. Too many professionals ignore these techniques and get stuck doing things that have short-term benefit (like accepting the first job offer they get), but don't ultimately deliver true happiness. It would be like taking a job to please your parents, only to realize ten years later that you've been branded as an expert in a field you abhor. By making an investment in learning the art of networking early in your career, you can ensure this scenario doesn't happen to you.

It can take years to make, grow, and keep the types of business relationships that will produce results. That's why we encourage you to start early in your career because if you wait, it will still take years. Establishing a professional network that can, and will, bring opportunities needs to be part of your lifestyle. It is a marathon, not a sprint. But when you run life's race with other cool people it makes everything better.

1

PEOPLE WANT TO WORK WITH PEOPLE THEY KNOW AND LIKE

We're going to let you in on a little secret: people want to work with people they know and like. Now, this is not to say that everyone who knows you and likes you wants to work with you. Your roommate sees enough of you as it is! But people would rather work with someone they like rather than a moody genius with a 4.0 GPA.

The most successful people are those who make networking a priority. The reason for this is that the more people you know, the better your chances are that some of those people will like you and want to help you. And the most efficient way to meet people is to network.

Your network should consist of people you know *and* like, and who feel the same way about you. These are the folks who will go out of their way to help you. Surround yourself with these people and never miss an opportunity to offer them assistance when you are able. This is how strong relationships are created. Chances are, if you master the art of building strong relationships, you will never be out of a job.

A successful career requires a network

While some people still spend an entire career at one company, this is definitely not the norm in today's labor market. According to a study from the U.S. Bureau of Labor Statistics, people between the ages of 18 and 42 should prepare to change employers (or jobs within the same company) an average of ten times over the course of a single career. Regardless of whether you spend 30 years at one company or three years at 10 companies, your network will be a critical part of your success.

Over the years as you develop and grow as a professional, your network will grow and develop too. You will evolve together. The ways in which you leverage your network at various stages of your career will vary as well. For example, at the beginning of your career, your network will be crucial to helping you find a job. Through referrals or network-ing contacts that you turn into recommendations, you will learn about job openings in what is often called "the hidden job market." The hidden job market consists of employ-ment opportunities you won't come across on any online job board, company website, or newspaper. We'll discuss specific methods for cultivating referrals and tapping into this market in Chapter 4.

Once you start working, your networking focus will shift from meeting people who can help you find a job to devel-oping friendships with professionals who can offer insights into your particular career field. You will join trade organi-zations or associations and start attending their events. In Chapter 6 we'll teach you the secrets on how to best lever-age your time when you are attending a networking event. "Working a room" can sound contrived, but the manner in which you engage other people in conversation can make all the difference in how you build long-term relationships going forward.

As you become more accomplished, your purpose for networking will change again. Your priority will be placed on networking with colleagues within your own company. At this stage you will likely have your sights set on career advancement and it will become critical that you are acknowledged for your professional achievements. In other words, once you get good at what you do, it's important that other people recognize your talent otherwise your chances of being promoted decrease. The importance of networking with fellow employees will become tantamount to the quality of the work you produce.

After many years of hard work, you may find yourself a leader in your field. The focus of your networking efforts will now extend beyond your own employer to competitors and peripheral or emerging markets. Why is it important to spend time rubbing elbows with the competition? You can be assured that in conversations with bosses, clients, potential customers and others, your competitors' names will be tossed about. It is in your best interest to already know their strengths and weaknesses. Networking with your competitors provides you access to this information first-hand. Knowing your competition takes some of the fear out of competing with them.

As you can see, the focus of your networking efforts may change as your career progresses, but the need to continuously sharpen your networking skills will remain consistent as long as you want to be successful.

The many faces of networking

Networking will play a significant role in both your personal and professional life. In fact, it already does. From your earliest days on the playground you began making connections and forging friendships. The people with whom you have surrounded yourself up to now make up your basic network. The proof that networking has already impacted your life is all around you in the form of your friends, family, teachers, coaches, neighbors, co-workers and classmates.

As you move forward, the people you choose to network with will continue to influence you. Here are just a few examples of how connecting with others has enhanced the lives of college students and recent graduates just like you:

- Kristin, from Southern Methodist University in Dallas, found two internships and her first post-college job through people she met at her church.

- Michael, a doctoral student at the University of Chicago, needed a cheap place to stay while he completed a research paper in upstate New York. A classmate of his was able to arrange for him to live rent free at her family's farm.

- Karyn learned about her job as the manager of alumni relations for the Melbourne Business School in Melbourne, Australia through her alumni club.

Networking Defined

What exactly is networking? It's no surprise that networking is a word that many recent graduates misunderstand because most colleges don't teach it. Even more college graduates shy away from networking because they have a preconceived notion about it. They envision "networking" as those uncomfortable events at which a hungry mob of strangers gathers around a half-empty buffet table and makes awkward attempts at small talk. And while yes, networking can be like this, it doesn't have to be.

If approached with the right attitude, networking can be a way to not only advance your career, but to form new friendships as well. Of course, some grads miss the point of networking entirely. The idea is to make connections, not transactions. If you take a genuine interest in others and help people reach their goals, you'll be successful.

A good network is also going to be vital to your personal growth because it serves as a constant source of inspiration and encouragement. Investing the time to develop a robust network early in your career will give you a huge advantage over your less motivated peers. Taking time to build your network is also just a fun way to kick off your career.

A network is having a lot of people who know and respect you, and understand your goals. It is then easy for them to refer you to potential employers, or recommend you for other opportunities because you are first in their mind when a relevant need arises. By the same token, you understand their goals and look for ways to help them. A network is a give-and-take arrangement.

Building a network takes a big commitment, and many recent graduates make the false assumption that their time is better spent sending out hundreds of résumés rather than making new contacts. They claim that they are too busy looking for a job to focus on anything other than résumés and cover letters, but by doing so they forget about the future. Many graduates have had life-changing career opportunities presented to them by people they knew well. But they wouldn't have learned about these opportunities if they hadn't taken the time away from writing cover letters to interact with their friends.

If you are a recent graduate of a well-known business school, you were probably introduced to networking early on; relationships with classmates and alumni are an important part of why people select certain universities for advanced degrees. There are many MBAs who keep in close contact with their classmates, and you can be sure that when a CEO from one of the top B-Schools moves to a new company, members of his or her network will follow.

The Networking Quotient

The first step towards improving your networking skills is to understand your strengths and weaknesses. It's also nice to know how your networking skills compare to those of your peers. Many people mistakenly believe that others share similar views and practices when it comes to networking. An avid networker thinks everyone takes relationships seriously, while the reluctant networker might assume everyone sees the practice as overrated and bothersome.

To make any strides in this area, or any area of your life, you need to make a realistic assessment of where you are starting. Then you need to know in which areas and how to improve. Without this knowledge you will never know if you are making any progress. For this reason, Thom created The Networking Quotient Quiz. This free, 30-question, on-line quiz will take you only eight minutes to complete. As you answer the questions, try hard to provide *your* answer, not the *right* answer.

The quiz allows you to assess how you react in a variety of networking situations. Moments after you answer the last question, you will receive your score and a comparison to others in your demographic area.

You can take the quiz whenever you like at *www.networkingquotient.com,* but to get the most from your test results, we suggest you put this book down now and complete the quiz before you continue reading.

Networking Myths

Now that we've talked about what networking *is*, let's take a closer look at what networking *is not*. Networking is not a simple game of connect-the-dots between whom you know and whom others know. Using a friend's name without their consent can jeopardize both relationships. You may think that once you have established a close relationship with someone, his or her network is automatically your network. Not true. Networking is not something you can do by yourself; it takes the participation and conscious help of others.

Here are several more myths about networking:

Myth 1: Networking is only for times when you are not busy.

Reality: There seems to be a boom-and-bust mentality around networking. People think that when they're happily employed they can ignore everyone around them. Conversely, when rumors of layoffs start, those people rally and try to pick up where they left off. In reality, if you fail to cultivate a relationship it will wither away. Jumping back into networking makes you seem flighty. As long as you have to eat lunch, schedule it with someone that you want to keep in touch with.

Myth 2: Only senior executives need a network.

Reality: Everyone can benefit from having a professional network. This is especially true for young professionals just starting out. For your future job, current position, or opportunities down the road, you must build your reputation, skills, and relationships now. No matter what your level, industry or job function, affiliations with others only have an upside. And remember, while networking, you are not only representing your employer, you are representing yourself. If your employer won't support your networking efforts by giving you the time and resources to join organizations and attend meetings (shame on them!), find a way to make it happen on your own. Your career is worth the investment.

Myth 3: The people you meet networking are never helpful.

Reality: If you do for others, most of them will return the favor. While the payoff may not be immediate, remember that the real reward is in developing a new relationship. Over the years we have had many experiences where people we met through networking have directly given us business, referred business to us, recruited us to better jobs or become some of our closest friends. Case in point: one of Thom's children has a godmother whom he met at a networking event.

Myth 4: Networking is unnecessary because if your GPA is high enough, the campus career center will find a job for you.

Reality: This is never true. While you may be more eligible for certain jobs from companies that are recruiting on campus, no one is going to find a position for you. More likely than not, the counselors at the career center don't even know you exist. Now might be a good time to start networking with them!

Myth 5: Decision makers never attend networking events.

Reality: Everyone goes somewhere. While the people you want to meet (i.e. hiring managers) might not be at the same events that you attend, they are not all hermits. Additionally, other people in their firms or in their networks just might be there, and you may have a chance to get an introduction through someone else.

Myth 6: Networking events sponsored by a particular organization are all the same. If the first one was a waste of time, there is no point in going back.

Reality: The chances are slim that you met everyone who belongs to the organization at one event. People lead busy lives and cannot possibly attend every event, no matter how committed to networking they are. Remember, it only takes one person who knows about the perfect job opportunity for you to change your life. Don't let one bad event keep you from meeting that one person.

Take Aways

People want to work with people they know and like.

A successful career requires a network.

Networking is a way of life, not something you do on days that you have extra time.

2

NETWORKING 101: THE BASICS

Building a network can be a powerful path to long-term career success. It's not about going out into the world and meeting people who will immediately hire you or hand over career opportunities. If it were that easy, everyone would be doing it. Rather than be of the mindset that everyone you meet should and will impact your career, view networking as an ongoing process where you meet people, get to know them and assist them when you can, never knowing who will come through for you in the long run.

Three Common Networking Personas

There are three broad categories of networkers:

1. Naturals

   You know those people who have contact lists longer than the Nile? It doesn't matter if you're looking for a place to live, a plumber or an exotic bird trainer; these people always seem to know a guy (or gal!). We call these folks naturals because meeting new people and building relationships comes easily to them. They have an inherent curiosity about others. They began connecting others long before they understood what networking even was. Naturals just enjoy being around others and, more often than not, others enjoy being in their company too.

Naturals share many characteristics aside from their large networks. They tend to be extroverts who are equally comfortable in large or small groups. Easily approachable, naturals are often quick to revive stalled conversations with their entertaining anecdotes. You know you've been in the presence of a natural networker when you walk away reenergized and with the names of five people you've "just got to meet"!

Thom Says

Several years ago I went to the wedding of a kindergarten classmate. It was amazing how many childhood friends the groom, then in his early 40s, had in attendance. While the groom and I are not as close today as we were in Miss O'Brien's class, I cannot recall a time when he was not my friend. The groom is a good example of a natural networker.

2. Uncomfortable Networkers

Networking does not come as easily to these people but they've bought into the idea and know they must network to grow their careers. They work to make meeting other people a priority. It's a little harder for them to make interpersonal connections but they succeed by working hard at it and over time they find it's no longer painful.

Uncomfortable networkers also have certain characteristics in common. They tend to be more introverted than natural networkers but are not necessarily shy. Uncomfortable networkers function better in small groups and favor talking one-on-one. Knowing when and how to break into conversations makes them anxious and so they sometimes just avoid introducing themselves altogether.

Anne Says

Early in my career I attended networking events with a particular colleague of mine. She had this amazing ability to move graciously from one group of people to the next. Unfailingly, the day following the event, she would show up to the office with a large stack of business cards. And she could remember some fact about every person she had met. While we were having lunch one day I made a comment about what a natural networker she was. She started laughing and practically fell out of her chair. She said, "Have you ever noticed that I wear a turtleneck sweater at these events? I get so nervous that I break out in hives. But I know that in order to do my job well networking has to be a part of my life. So, I've learned to adapt."

I will never forget that conversation. It made me realize that anyone can learn how to network effectively.

3. Selfish Networkers. These people are annoyed by those who cannot help them.

Many selfish people do become very successful, and they never acknowledge that others have contributed to their success. We all know people like this: their sole interaction is with those from whom they seek immediate payoff.

Successful people build networks by cultivating true, long-lasting relationships. Building solid business relationships with a "What's in it for me?" mentality just doesn't work. People either know and trust you, or they don't. Because a relationship is solidified over a long period of time, networkers with purely selfish motives will eventually be found out and dismissed.

Leslie Says

Maria calls me once a year, unfailingly. We go to coffee and she pumps me for consulting leads, never returning the favor. I go because she is pee-in-your-pants funny and I find her outlook on life and stories hilarious. But I don't expect anything else from her other than an hour's worth of entertainment.

Why people don't network

Some people are so overwhelmed by the amount of effort that networking will take that they simply choose to avoid it. Rarely do those people achieve the level of success that they would have reached had they expended the energy to expand their circle of influence. Here are some additional reasons people avoid networking:

> **I'm too busy.** While it is true that there is little free time in life these days, time spent building a network of contacts is an investment in your future.

> **I'm set in my ways.** I'd rather spend my time with my girlfriend or riding my bike rather than put myself out there.

> **Am I worthy?** Self-doubt is another excuse for avoiding connecting with others. This is silly, of course, because the point of networking is showing others what you can bring to the table. People want to know who you are. If you prove that you are reliable, and intend to contribute to others' success in addition to your own, people will want to know you, even executives at the highest levels. Consider the following story about a CEO and his views on networking.

Bryan is the CEO of his fourth technology start-up. He is often approached to join the Young Presidents' Organization or networking groups for senior executives. Instead, he started a group made up of individuals of all levels in marketing, sales, law, and insurance. He also included some entrepreneurs. His theory was that his company's needs might not always be solved by someone who was his peer, but that a cross-section of people in business would bring many good connections and points of view that he might not otherwise be exposed to. This group met monthly for two years and at each meeting every attendee had to talk about what his or her largest challenge was that month. Help often came from the least expected person. If, for example, a company needed a new receptionist, another CEO would never sing the praises of his own receptionist, but a sales person or HR executive just might do so to help their friend, the receptionist, find a better opportunity. Bryan believed that having your network go from top to bottom was more helpful than just knowing those on top.

The Four Steps of Networking

Developing professional relationships through networking is a process that takes an extraordinary amount of time and effort. In the months after college, when you're preoccupied with starting an exciting new chapter in your life, adding networking activities to your already overloaded schedule can be daunting. Even for the most motivated graduates, it's hard to know where to start. Fortunately, the phases of building mutually beneficial relationships through networking actually evolve quite naturally.

Step 1: Introduce

The first step is just making a simple introduction. This could be introducing yourself to a new contact at an event, in a meeting, through a mutual friend, on a social networking website, or via phone or email. While this may seem obvious, keep in mind that how you are perceived during the introduction step of networking will impact your future relationship with this person. Be conscious of your actions and strive to make a good impression. Your goal is to come across as a person others will want to get to know.

The introduction is your one and only chance to make a positive first impression. Here are a few pointers:

- As you introduce yourself, remember to pronounce your full name clearly. This is especially important for people with unusual names. If you do not catch the name of the person you are meeting, ask them to repeat it immediately, as it will save you from an embarrassing situation later on.

- Smile and be approachable. Use eye contact and a firm handshake to convey confidence. This will ensure you project a mature and professional image.

- Dress appropriately for the occasion. When in doubt about the dress code, wear something a notch or two nicer than what you think is required. It's always better to overdress than to wind up underdressed.

- Have a few conversation starters ready to go, in case the conversation stalls immediately after names are exchanged.

- If you are in a meeting, do your research and be prepared. For example, if you are meeting with someone who accepted your request for an informational interview, have your questions ready and know what company and in which department he or she works.

- If you are introducing yourself to someone online, via email or by phone, get to the point quickly. Plan what you want to say and be up front about your purpose in contacting them. Don't fumble around with words, or be vague. If you're nervous, or worried that you might be when the time comes, write down what you want to say. To avoid sounding like you're reading from a script, just jot down a few bullet points that will help you stay on track during your introduction.

Step 2: Share

The sharing step of networking is your chance to exchange information that will help forge a connection. It is vitally important that you possess the ability to talk about yourself succinctly and in a way that makes people want to know more. Your goal is to keep the conversation going long enough to find something in common and establish rapport.

It is not at all unusual for a couple of simple questions to completely stump people as they are chatting with someone new or at an event. Questions as common as "What do you want to do?" or "What types of companies have you been interviewing with?" can tongue tie even the most intelligent graduates. Practice your answers until you become as comfortable responding to them as you are putting on your socks in the morning.

Never lose sight of the fact that the sharing step of networking involves two people. Often, people are so focused on making a good impression that they fail to listen to anything the other person says. To build mutually beneficial relationships, which are, after all, the entire reason you're networking, you must discover the goals and passions of the people you're meeting. You will find that asking open-ended, compelling questions, as well as sharing your experiences, will lead your conversations into territory that is useful to all parties.

Connections can be on a personal or professional level, so feel free to ask questions outside of business. In fact, some of the most successful business relationships were started when people discovered they had a common personal interest, and vice versa.

"When I was looking for my first real job, I sent out exactly 92 résumés. I applied for any job that had anything to do with computers: helpdesk, PC tech, web design, programming, etc. My 92 résumés resulted in two callbacks and no offers.

One day I was in the college computer lab working on a programming project. One of my classmates was there, too, and approached me for some help. He asked what I did for work. A little embarrassed, I told him that I was working at KFC, but trying to get into IT. He mentioned that he worked with CKE Enterprises (Carl's Jr/Hardee's) in the IT department as a desktop engineer and said that he knew of help desk jobs that were open at the company and even offered to pick up an application for me. At the next class he brought the application which I filled out and dropped off at their corporate headquarters. A few days later I had my first interview and got the job. The 92 résumés didn't even make a dent against the power of a network."

Jonathon Unger
CEO, SmallCart Systems
Los Angeles, CA

Step 3: Build

Build is the step where most networkers fumble because this is where the follow-up happens. It takes both a time commitment and a healthy supply of creativity. Even the most seasoned and natural networkers often drop the ball when it comes to this step.

Sometimes it's obvious how to follow up with a new networking contact. For example, you are introduced to someone who has agreed to look over your résumés and offer you feedback. You would send them a pleasant email, thank them for their assistance, and of course, attach your résumés. More times than not, however, it's unclear how a relationship will evolve, and you may be uncertain of how, or even if, you will be able to help one another. Here are a few strategies to keep in mind:

- Reach out within a few days of initially meeting someone, as they are most likely to still remember you at that point. You can send an email, call on the phone, or compose a handwritten note and send it through snail mail. There doesn't have to be a need-based reason for contacting them; getting in touch to say "it was nice to meet you" is enough.

- Do something to keep the connection alive and blossoming. With time and multiple interactions, you may well discover common ground or the opportunity to work together on a project. If you are attending another networking event that might be of interest to them, invite them along. If you know someone that your new contact could benefit from knowing, offer to make the introduction.

- Look for ways to help them first. Make it second nature to give of yourself before asking others to assist you.

- Look for organizations, events, or newspaper articles that you think might interest that person and pass the information along. If something newsworthy happens to them or their company, send a note with your congratulations; it shows you're paying attention!

- Be prepared to let go. Not all relationships will develop into anything substantial or worthwhile. Sometimes the interest is not mutual, or opportunities to reconnect just don't happen. It's usually not personal or a sign that the person doubts your talents. Move on, and focus on the relationships with people in your network that are evolving and growing.

To really build relationships takes time; this means months to some and years to others. Therefore, one of the most important personal traits you need to successfully build a working network is patience. More often than not, people want you to prove yourself before you join their inner circle. Just as you would not invite a near-stranger to Thanksgiving dinner at your home, people do not welcome you into their network after an initial meeting. Let the relationship develop at its own pace. Follow up, but don't try to force a friendship.

Step 4: Maintain

Sometimes we take for granted the people we know best and assume they will be around to assist us when we need them. Likewise, we assume they will ask us for help when they need it. The access to online networking tools—such as the "contacts" feature on *LinkedIn*, or the "friends" list on *Facebook*—makes us somewhat complacent about this step. Don't confuse updating your status with maintaining relationships with the people in your network. Every relationship needs some attention, and you don't want to lose an important ally due to negligence.

Set a goal to proactively connect with key members in your network. It should be every three to four months on average; at the more critical stages in your career it will be more often. You do not have to meet in person with every one of these people; that would not be practical or a wise use of everyone's time. Staying in touch via email, phone, and online will suffice. The key is to be consistent, to hold yourself accountable, and to make the effort.

Thom Says

In a tough economy, the people who usually fare better are the ones who have maintained their networks by staying in touch, staying visible, and making time to assist others that have reached out.

A few years ago I got a call from a friend of a friend. This woman had always discredited networking and thought it was only for people with free time. She had been laid off from a large computer manufacturer in Austin and was not having any luck finding new employment. Two months had passed and, with a slow job market, she saw no prospects for employment. Many of her co-workers had already landed in new positions, and she discovered that all of them had found their opportunities through someone they knew.

Now that she needed a job, she was behind candidates who had an "in" for the few coveted openings. And so we had coffee. It quickly became clear that she was a person who did not know how to maintain a network. One of the first rules is to respect the others in your network. Here is what happened:

She invited me out and expected me to pick up the check since I was employed. *If you invite someone to coffee or lunch you should expect to pick up the bill. If the person offers to pay, you can decide if it is appropriate, but do not assume that because you are out of work your guest should buy your lunch.*

She was not grateful for my time. I had never met this woman before and yet I spent an hour listening to her situation. *Networking is not free therapy. She mistakenly assumed that since I was a natural networker, our time together was no big deal.* She never said thank you when we parted. I never received any follow up from her and, not surprisingly, I have never seen her again.

No one will do it for you

No matter how much you may want to, networking is not a task you can delegate. You are the only person who can build your network. To gain the benefits that a network offers, you must invest the time to meet people and get to know them.

Thom Says

Barbara, an attorney who had recently passed the bar, joined the law firm where I worked as the marketing manager. She told me that while she wanted to grow her practice quickly, she did not want to invest any time or energy into networking as her workload was staggering already. She wanted me to do some things to make her phone ring. Her belief was that our firm should run advertisements on her specialty, and that if there were ads, people would call her directly. I explained to her that advertising was a tool to give the firm some recognition and that knowing the name of the firm would help them to connect with her. But to win in a relationship sales environment, she needed to build relationships, and there were no shortcuts. She needed to build that trust.

To come out on top in a business where relationships win the business, you need to start early and keep at it. Those at the top of the relationship game have a combination of a great reputation for the work they do, and they establish lasting relationships. They work hard at both. Work hard on networking? Yes!

The Fun Factor

All this talk about the amount of time and effort that go into building a strong network can take the focus off the fact that this should be fun. For naturally gregarious people, making friends and building long-lasting, mutually beneficial relationships is just part of daily life. For people who are more introverted, the level of attention it takes to do such things can be tedious. And for those intensely shy graduates who prefer to meet new people through email only, networking can be downright painful. But if you are convinced that having a network can and will benefit your career, you might as well have a good time in the process, regardless of the amount of effort it requires.

Most people have an interesting story to tell. Think of this as unraveling an amazing puzzle. People like to and will talk about themselves. Learn where they grew up, where they went to college. Have they traveled extensively? How did their career path lead them to where they are today? Are they married? Do they have children? It's easy to become so focused on someone's professional attributes that we forget that they are more than just the CFO of a manufacturing

company. Treat your interactions with others as an explora-
tion. Each day, try to learn one thing new about someone.
Consider it your own secret game.

Many of the events you will attend are social in nature.
People come to these social events looking to network and
enjoy themselves. When people inquire how you're doing,
have ready a *positive* response, even if you're having a lousy
day. If asked how the job search is going, give a response
like "It's been a great learning experience so far, and I look
forward to finding a great position." Steer clear of negative
responses like, "It stinks, no one's hiring, and I'm totally
frustrated." Here's the thing: if you come across as negative,
people won't stick around to talk to you for very long. Even
if you are having an uncharacteristically bad day, try to stay
positive when you're speaking with others. The optimism
in your voice speaks louder than anything else you can say.

Take Aways

*You cannot rush through or skip any of the four
steps of networking: introduce, share, build,
maintain.*

*If you make the effort, you will be more successful
than the people who choose not to network at all.*

No one can network for you.

3

THE BLUEPRINT: HOW TO GET

STARTED IN NETWORKING

Around graduation time it seems as though *everyone* is talking about how important it is to network. "It's the only way to get hired in this economy." "That's how so-and-so got his job." And, "Your résumés won't even get looked at unless you know someone at the company." These are phrases heard repeatedly from well-meaning friends and family. What's frustrating is that no one seems able to explain exactly how you're supposed to *get started* networking. Where do you go? How do you break into established networks? What do you say to the new people you meet?

While networking can be intimidating at first, it helps to remember that you are about to meet some exciting and interesting people. As you start your networking journey, remind yourself how much you stand to gain and that many people do not take the time to build a network so you are already that much ahead of the game. To give yourself the best chance of succeeding as you make the transition from college to career, here are some strategies you can use to make your networking efforts more productive right from the start.

Building Your Personal Brand

The concept of personal branding has received intense attention in recent years, especially as it relates to introducing oneself to employers via social networking. But self-packaging and self-promotion is not only for online networking activities. How you come across in person is ultimately going to be the deciding factor in whether or not you land the job.

Your personal brand has already been created. It encompasses everything you've ever said or done, and it's critical to recognize now that your actions are an integral part of how others perceive you.

While we all make mistakes, it's important to take responsibility for your actions and move on, exerting more control over certain aspects of your behavior if necessary. People are forgiving if they believe you have made necessary changes and see that you do not repeat your mistakes. If there are things you need to change, don't be too hard on yourself, just acknowledge what you will do differently in the future and move on. For example, if you are habitually late for appointments, commit to being on time going forward. If you have a tendency to cancel meetings or outings with others at the last minute, make a mental note to stop doing that immediately. All of these actions, along with your personal appearance and vocal presentation, make up your personal brand.

Now that the lines between our personal and professional lives have been blurred thanks to the insertion of technology into every aspect of our lives, it's no longer feasible to compartmentalize the two. Employers will look at your

Facebook page and they will see what you've been tweeting about. Your digital footprint should be one that complements your offline self. Remove anything from any online profiles that would give someone the wrong impression. Once an employer has seen a photo of you throwing down margaritas on spring break in your yellow polka dot bikini, it's hard for them to take you seriously.

Personal Branding Assessment

Building and continuously improving your personal brand is the best first step you can take when getting started networking. To help assess where you are, here are 12 questions to ask yourself. Take as much time as you need to compose your answers before continuing on.

1. Do I dress appropriately depending on the occasion and location? Would others agree?

2. Do I treat others with respect? Would others agree?

3. Do I give every job or project my best effort? Would others agree?

4. Do I follow through with my promises? Would others agree?

5. Do I look for ways to help others? Would others agree?

6. Do I give off positive or negative energy? How would others describe my attitude on most days?

Now let's take a look at your answers and how that information can help you improve your personal brand.

1. *Do I dress appropriately depending on the occasion and location?*

People judge you based on a first impression. According to the image experts, it takes approximately three seconds for someone to form their first impression of you. Often, during the first three seconds of meeting someone, you haven't yet uttered a single word. So, fair or not, you are going to be judged in part on how you are dressed. And if you are not dressed appropriately, you will start at a disadvantage.

People are going to assume you're as sharp as you dress so don't skimp on professional attire. When you are just starting out in your career you will set yourself apart from your peers and other job candidates by looking well put together. You will also feel more confident if you look professional, which in turn will make you act more confident.

Dressing well is almost always rewarded. Take Joel for example. Soon after landing a job in finance, Joel realized he needed to dress better. He decided to use some of the money he had saved up to buy a very nice suit. Not too long after, his boss chose three employees to take to a business lunch. Not three *entry-level* employees mind you, just three employees. Guess who was invited? During that lunch Joel made some very intelligent points that made the boss take more of an interest in Joel's future at the company. What landed Joel on the boss's radar in the first place was the fact that he dressed well.

Of course, you don't want to be overdressed either. Although it's better to be overdressed than underdressed, you can send the wrong message if you overdo it. Once you start working, keep in mind that how other people dress at your level may not be the appropriate dress code. Look above you, not next to you, for fashion tips. We have always found "dress for the position above you" to be good advice.

2. *Do I treat others with respect? Would others agree?*

Regardless of someone's job function, treat everyone you meet with respect. Though a certain structural hierarchy may exist within your company that gives you authority over some people, or vice versa, remember that people within that hierarchy are human beings. You'll get better results by treating others as people rather than titles.

Additionally, since it's impossible to predict the future, you have no way of knowing which networking contacts, co-workers, or classmates may eventually be on the other side of the hiring equation from you. If you treat everyone as you would like to be treated, it's more than likely that you will be regarded favorably in the future.

Here are a few things to bear in mind:

- Assume that everyone you work with has good intentions and is doing the best they can.
- Give people the benefit of the doubt when they make a mistake.
- Give credit where it's due.
- Say hello to people that you pass in the common areas at internships, networking events, and at work, even if you don't know who they are.
- Be a good listener; show interest when someone is speaking, and don't interrupt people.

3. *Do I give every job or project my best effort? Would others agree?*

You must work hard if you hope to be successful. It's that simple. Work hard and don't expect immediate praise or for every good deed to be noticed in the short term. Remember it's long-term success that you're shooting for. You'll accomplish more and earn more respect if you care more about getting the job done than you do about who gets the credit. Each time you complete a task, ask yourself if it was truly the best you could do. If your answer is no, do it again.

When you are just starting out, you need to be perceived as someone who is willing to go above and beyond the call of duty. Accept assignments that require you to work overtime. On the other hand, don't take on more than you can reasonably handle. Once you are seen as lazy it is very difficult to change people's perceptions of you. It is much better to start your career on overdrive than by coasting along in neutral. Push yourself as hard as you can in the beginning of your career. Get as much experience as possible and never turn down an opportunity to learn from people more experienced than you. Even if you're staying late to make copies for an executive, use that time to ask them questions about how they got to where they are. Then, when you've pushed yourself as far as you think you can go, push harder.

4. *Do I follow through with my promises? Would others agree?*

Building a personal brand is, more than anything, about credibility. One of the fastest ways to ruin your credibility is to go back on a promise, however insignificant it may seem. For example, if you say you will send a link to an article to someone you met at a networking event, make sure you do it, preferably before they email you to remind you. People who consistently do what they promise achieve better success in networking than people who project a largely fabricated image.

5. *Do I look for ways to help others? Would others agree?*

Are you having regular conversations with your peers, friends, and business contacts about their goals and looking for ways to help them? If not, this is something you should start doing now. People are generally more receptive to helping people they know would help them if the situation were reversed. Therefore, being someone who is always on the lookout for ways to help the people in your network is a good way to improve the odds of the favor being returned one day.

6. *Do I give off positive or negative energy? How would others describe my attitude on most days?*

Much of your success will be determined by your reactions to situations. People like to be around positive people, not those who are a mental drain. Graduates with a can-do attitude inspire those around them. Are people likely to describe you as someone who always has something uplifting to say, or someone with something to complain about? With just your attitude, you have the power to lift people's spirits, as well as your own.

Each morning, take a few deep breaths to center yourself. Then greet your day with an open mind and positive attitude. Go into your meetings with the intention to be a part of the solution, not the problem. Surround yourself with people who energize and inspire you. Don't be quick to assume the worst about a situation or person. And if you have to deliver bad news, find a positive note to end on. If something happens to dampen your spirits during the day, take a few more deep breaths to re-center yourself and look at the situation from a different perspective. Remember that you choose your attitude.

Taking Your Personal Brand to the Next Level

Once you have given some thought to the questions above you will be one step closer to building a strong brand because you'll have identified the areas you need to work on. Here are a few more things you can do to take your personal brand to the next level:

- Volunteer for business and charitable organizations that you have a genuine interest in.
- Mentor others.

- Improve your public speaking skills.
- Ask people you trust and respect for honest feedback and advice.
- Refer business to those in your network.
- Write articles for business or trade publications.

Setting Your Networking Goals

Where are you on your career path today? Where would you like to be in five years? Ten years? Knowing where you're going is a critical element in figuring out how to get there and understanding how networking can help you get there. But, if you do not have a complete vision of what you want from your career yet, don't sweat it. You are not alone.

Jobs and careers change, and new opportunities can arise at any time, so you need to remain flexible with your networking goals anyway. That being said, identifying specific goals can help you reach your career aspirations and find the job of your dreams sooner than you can without them.

Create a series of short- and long-term goals

You've probably heard that in order to be successful you need to have goals. We believe that's true. Goal setting is a process we advise every young professional to devote time to and take seriously. But did you know that some people set goals more effectively than others?

When it comes to setting goals, there are three types to be familiar with:

> **Short-term.** Short-term goals can usually be achieved within a few weeks or months. These goals can often be reached sooner by prioritizing your time carefully and limiting distractions. Some examples include: reading one book each month; taking two industry-related courses each year; completing the continuing education necessary to maintain your professional certifications or acquiring new ones. Setting short-term goals enables you to create a realistic timeline for achieving your long-term career aspirations. It helps you stay motivated and achieve success faster because you are able to celebrate the accomplishment of several milestones along the way. This makes achieving your dreams more methodical and less overwhelming.
>
> **Long-term.** Long-term goals generally take several months or years to accomplish, and as a rule, there's not much you can do to speed up the time required to achieve them. Some examples of long-term goals include: becoming a doctor; repairing bad credit; saving money for a down payment on a house. Once you know what your long-term goals are, it will be easier to identify networking opportunities that will bring you closer to achieving them.

Specific. Specific goals are clearly defined and provide little room for misinterpretation. Examples include: find an entry-level logistics position in the next six months with a large company; have an article published in a particular newsletter; learn to use Adobe Photoshop. By setting specific goals you create benchmarks that you are able to use to measure your success. For example, did you learn Adobe Photoshop in the time frame you set for yourself? If not, what did you learn that you can apply toward your next attempt? When you use less specific wording, it's too easy to make excuses for failing to achieve the goal. For example, let's say you decide your goal is to find a job. Without including the specific parameter of "a job in logistics at a large company", you would determine that any job you got meant you had succeeded in reaching your goal of finding a job. Yet, you would be unhappy because what you really wanted was a job in logistics.

Now that you are familiar with the types of goals you need to set, let's look at the five-step process for actually achieving them.

Step 1: Identify your goals.

It's important to identify and make lists of long-term, short-term, and specific goals.

Step 2: Write them down.

Write your goals down on a piece of paper, or in a notebook, and put them somewhere where you can refer to them regularly.

Step 3: Check your phrasing. Is it specific enough?

Goals such as "I want to have a successful career" are too vague to offer much in the way of motivation and direction. Remember, the purpose of crafting specific goals is to give you a way to measure your success and keep you accountable when benchmarking your progress. Write down precisely what you intend to accomplish and when you plan to achieve it.

Step 4: Keep your goals where you can view them frequently.

You may want to tape them to your bathroom mirror, or put them on the visor in your car. Just keep them visible so that you are consistently reminded how attainable your dream is.

Step 5: Celebrate each success, no matter how small.

Be sure to celebrate each time you reach one of your goals. This will help you stay motivated, even though the journey to your ultimate goal seems long.

Thom's System:

At the beginning of each year I write down my goals. Then I laminate them and keep them in my wallet where I'll frequently see them.

Anne's System

Every six months I write a vision statement in a special journal I keep next to my bed. My vision statement is more or less an outline of what I want in my life for the next year. Then I make a list of the goals I need to reach in order to achieve my vision. Before I go to sleep, I flip through my list to check my progress and add notes here and there to keep me motivated.

Identify specific networking goals

It's also important to have a specific set of goals for how you're going to start networking. Since we all have our own unique strengths and weaknesses, it makes sense that we'd all have different networking goals. For example, a short-term goal for someone with social anxiety might be to attend one networking event in the next month. For someone who is comfortable in social situations, a short-term goal might be to attend at least one networking event each week. Another short-term goal for this person could be to meet five new people at each event and work toward building a long-term relationship with at least one of those five.

The point is to set goals that are realistic for you and your needs at this stage of your career.

To give you some more ideas as you develop your own list of networking goals, here are sample goals for the uncomfortable and natural networking personas we discussed in Chapter 2.

Sample goals for uncomfortable networkers. Introverts tend to discredit or ignore networking activities because it's simply not in their nature to mingle. But just because you may be someone who doesn't necessarily enjoy social situations with a bunch of strangers, doesn't preclude you from becoming very successful networkers. If this sounds like you, your first short-term goal is just to put yourself out there. Go to the next networking event that comes your way. Just go. Getting out of your comfort zone is intensely empowering, and you will be amazed at how much easier networking becomes once the excuse of not attending is removed. Another short-term goal could be updating your *LinkedIn* profile and making sure it's 100% complete. Join some online networking groups just to get your feet wet. A long-term goal could be coming up with a schedule that includes at least a few networking events a month and not skipping any of them. Celebrate by doing something nice for yourself after you've attended a total of ten events.

Sample goals for natural networkers. Because natural networkers are usually outgoing by nature, it's not a stretch for them to attend events and feel at ease talking to new groups of people. If this describes you, a short-term goal could be to join a committee or help plan an upcoming event for one of the networking organizations you find most worthwhile. A long-term goal might be to join the leadership team for an organization that sponsors networking events you enjoy. See Chapter 6 for more about specific organizations that are great places for graduates to start networking.

The thought of networking terrified me when I started. At my first networking event, I was pleasantly surprised to run into someone I knew. On the other hand, I was horrified to learn that I would have to stand up and give a 30-second infomercial about my practice. Since I was the first to introduce myself, I had nothing to go by and I flopped! However, that experience motivated me to grow as a professional, and as a networker.

Several months later I attended another event. Due to inclement weather, only two other people showed up—the organizer and her friend. This turned out to be a wonderful opportunity to get to know both women on a more intimate level. The organizer invited me to give a talk at a future event, and her friend later presented me with a speaking opportunity as well. The moral of the story: show up!

Through networking I've met some exceptionally talented, passionate and motivated people who have enriched my life.

Julia Di Nardo, Ph.D., Psychologist
www.HealTheHunger.com
Montreal, QC, Canada

Making the Commitment

At the very beginning of your career, when you are just building your personal brand and even trying on different professional hats, don't cast a wide net when it comes to networking commitments. The reason for this is that you want to build a high level of trust with the new people you're meeting. You want to get to know these new contacts personally, not just casually. Therefore it's better to become very active in a few circles than to attempt to sporadically participate in several.

To stay motivated and committed to your networking goals, ask a friend or two to join you in your networking endeavors. Being with friends makes it much easier to follow through with attending events. This is an especially helpful strategy if you have friends in the same field as you.

If you make networking a priority, set your goals, create a plan, and make a commitment to follow through, then networking will eventually become a habit. You'll find that networking is very enjoyable once you get the hang of it, and that meeting new people will benefit you in ways you can't even imagine right now.

Evaluating the Plan

Every so often come back to your networking goals and see if anything has changed. For example, perhaps your current networking plan is made up of goals that will help you find a job. In a few months' time you may wish to revise your goals to be more consistent with a young professional looking to educate yourself about your field or industry. It actually helps to track your networking results.

The benefits of networking may not always seem apparent in the beginning, and even later on they are often intangible. Tracking your results will help keep you motivated. Consider keeping a networking diary or notebook. When you attend events and meet new people, jot down their names along with some notes about them to help you remember who they are and what you discussed. Additionally, include any ideas about how you might follow up with them. If you learn about a new networking group you should join, or if you hear about a company that is hiring, record these bits of information as well. It will help you determine which events and organizations are giving you the best contacts.

Neither Rome nor a network was built all in one day. Don't make the mistake of expecting to see results within a week of meeting somebody. Relationships are built over time as people get to know and trust you. The people you meet at networking events are not running back to their offices and searching for job openings or other leads to send to you. In fact, even someone who was very impressed by you may not have a viable opportunity to assist you for months or even years. Be patient and be consistent in your networking efforts; stay focused on the big picture.

While you do not want to keep score exactly, you do want to evaluate how the people in your network are helping you. Each of us only has a certain amount of time to invest in networking, and while we want to be courteous to everyone, there are selfish people out there who just never give back. You need to learn to identify these people, and the sooner the better. If you find yourself helping someone out quite a lot who never seems to have an opening in his calendar for you, focus your energies elsewhere.

Evaluate the organizations and events that you are involved in. Are you meeting the kinds of people you want to know at the events you are attending? Are you acquiring new skills, education, and leadership opportunities in your field?

If not, it may be time to join new organizations or networking groups, or find a way to make time spent in your current circles more beneficial.

Take Aways

Your personal brand is comprised of everything you say and do. Learn to manage your personal brand so that you make the best impression possible.

Write down your goals and keep them somewhere visible so you are reminded of what it is you want to achieve.

You must make the commitment to follow through with your networking efforts if you want to reach your goals.

4

THE NUTS AND BOLTS:

BUILDING RELATIONSHIPS

People who view their personal relationships and professional relationships very differently tend to feel a kinship toward their social friends but don't have the same affinity toward their business contacts. This can translate to your business contacts not being given the same consideration as your social friends. All people want to feel important and respected. If you treat business contacts as a means to an end, you will never develop the type of friendships that we encourage in this book.

Still others approach networking as if it's simply a numbers game. These folks will email anyone, ask for what they want and cross their fingers that somebody will come through for them. Have you ever received a mass email from someone you barely knew, asking you to do him or her a favor? If so, you've already experienced a numbers networker.

In this chapter we are going to explain why you need to put the same amount of effort into building and maintaining professional relationships as you do with your personal friendships. People don't stop being human when they walk into the office on Monday morning. If you care about the people you meet it shows, regardless of the situation. When you make other people feel important and respected, and let them know you care, they will be drawn to you. To successfully build any relationship requires effort, authenticity, respect, patience, and the occasional sacrifice. Only then will you be able to turn networking contacts into the most powerful resources you can have during a job search: referrals, recommendations, and references.

Your Approach Is Everything

Some people only start networking because they need a job. And while finding employment is one possible outcome of networking (we'll discuss several in this chapter), it should never be your sole reason for networking. To simply focus on whether or not someone can get you a job essentially tells them you think they have nothing else of value to offer.

Karyn, who has managed the alumni relations departments for two top-tier international graduate business schools, says, "I can't even count the number of emails I've had forwarded to me over the years from alumni who were offended that students—whom they have never met—wrote to them out of the blue asking for a job. The alumni are stunned. They ask me, 'Do they really think this approach is going to work?' I try to explain to the students it's like proposing marriage on a first date. It's completely inappropriate."

Instead of making the effort to build rapport with the alumni and by only focusing on their short-term need (a job), the students in Karyn's story miss the big picture of what networking is all about. We hope you won't make the same mistake. A better approach when contacting alumni, or anyone for that matter, is to focus on learning about an industry, gathering information, discovering how to transition into a different field; in short, it's about *asking questions*. Use this initial point of contact to start building ground for future interactions.

How You Are Perceived Determines How You Are Received

At the start of your career, you will likely do the majority of reaching out to potential networking contacts. As you gain experience in your field, people will begin to seek you out as well. For the purposes of this chapter, however, we're going to assume that you will be the one initiating contact.

Today, most professionals prefer to be contacted by email initially. It makes sense when you think about it; if someone you had never met called you on the phone unexpectedly and started asking you detailed questions about yourself and your career, how would that make you feel? A phone conversation is more intimate than an email exchange, and, until the relationship has progressed to a more familiar level, stick to email. There are always exceptions to the rule, but why take the chance of offending someone you're hoping to impress?

Sending an email is less intrusive, and a thoughtfully constructed email can work to your advantage if you compose it properly. Here are a few things to pay attention to when you are sending an email to a potential new contact:

Salutation. This is the first chance you have to make a good impression in an email. Don't blow it by spelling the person's name wrong. We've both received notes addressed to Tom or Ann. That tells us that whoever took the time to write to us didn't spend any time learning anything about us.

Tone. Striking the right tone is important when contacting someone you've never met. You don't want to be too casual, nor do you want to sound like a character from a Jane Austen novel either. The tone should be respectful, not demanding. You want to sound assertive, but not aggressive, and ambitious, but not pushy.

Length. Get to the point, quickly. That conveys that you understand the constraints on your contact's time and do not wish to impose. At the same time, be thorough. Introduce yourself, explain why you felt compelled to contact the person to whom you are writing, and state your desire for a follow-up meeting at their convenience. A length of no more than three paragraphs, consisting of four to five sentences each, should be sufficient to get your message across succinctly. Do not include any attachments, as opening them requires extra work on the receiver's end. You don't want to waste anyone's time. In addition, the person's company may filter emails from unknown addresses with attachments into a spam or junk folder. Thus, your email may never even reach the person for whom it is intended.

Grammar. Nothing says, "Don't take me seriously" as loudly as sloppy writing coupled with poor grammar. Avoid icons and abbreviations best suited for text messaging. Double-check your spelling and use of capitalization; aim for textbook-perfect grammar.

Many graduates make the mistake of asking their networking contacts for a job or a lead on a job, the first time they meet. By not doing so, you will stand out and make a good impression simply by not being so presumptuous. The pressure to find the job you need should not supersede the reality that a long-term relationship can be mutually beneficial.

New graduates with an "it's all about me" mindset miss out on all sorts of opportunities to develop relationships with people who could have a meaningful impact on their careers or lives down the road. During the course of an otherwise insignificant conversation someone might share a story or advice that resonates with you, causing you to alter your approach to a key aspect of your life. People tend to cross our paths for a reason, but it's up to you to discover why. When you attempt to pre-determine someone's role in your life by assuming they can only help you obtain a position at their company, for example, you risk eradicating the chance of a bigger and more meaningful relationship.

One-on-One Meetings Are a Gift

Sitting down with someone you have never met for a one-on-one meeting is the most effective way to build your relationship with that person, and you should view this opportunity as a precious gift. There are only 24 hours in a day, and any time that someone agrees to sit down with you is golden.

Meetings give you a chance to:

- Spend quality, focused time together without the distractions of crowds at networking events
- Learn about someone and their profession, and tell them about you
- Ask questions about how someone you admire got to where they are today
- Ask questions or discuss topics that may not be appropriate in the presence of others
- Strengthen your connection and build trust, credibility, and shared experiences

Additionally, consider how the other person is responding to you throughout the meeting. Watch their body language. Are they leaning forward in their seat, indicating they are engaged in the conversation, or do they appear bored? If it's the latter, don't ramble on. Perhaps it's time to move on to a new topic. On the other hand, if the person you're meeting with is very animated while discussing a certain topic, zone in on that and ask questions or tell a relevant story to establish common interests. Remember, their perception of you will determine how much credibility you'll have with them and whether future meetings are likely, so it's up to you to make certain the meeting goes smoothly.

Here are six tips to ensure your one-on-one meetings are successful:

1. **Be prepared.** Do your research so you can ask intelligent questions about the person and his or her company. Knowing someone's background always makes a good impression. Have an agenda and a few goals for what you want to get out of the meeting. Have your list of questions for the other person memorized or noted somewhere you can refer to them quickly if necessary. Try to work them into the conversation naturally instead of reading from a list. Remember that the main goal here is to build a relationship, not conduct an interrogation. Don't stay up too late the night before an important meeting and don't wait until the last minute to do your research. You're more likely to retain information if you've had some time to digest it.

2. **Be respectful.** Make the meeting as logistically convenient for the other person as possible. Meet according to their schedule and offer to meet somewhere close to where they work or live. If

someone has to drive across town to meet with you, you run a greater risk of their canceling than if you meet at the restaurant next to their office. If someone tells you a specific time that is best to meet, make it work. And there is no excuse for arriving late. Time is a precious resource and the best way to demonstrate your appreciation for the meeting is to arrive and depart as scheduled. Agree to the length of the meeting beforehand, and stick to it. It's helpful to confirm the meeting length when you first sit down. You can say, "I really appreciate your taking the time to meet with me today, are you still free for 45 minutes? This way, if something has changed, you can steer the meeting accordingly. Finally, people have certain comfort zones when it comes to what topics they are comfortable discussing. Honor those comfort zones. If they seem to stay away from certain topics, or request that you not ask about particular aspects of their business, don't ask.

3. **Be attentive.** Listen more than you speak. You will gain far more from listening than you ever will by talking. There is an old saying: you have two ears and one mouth, thus you should talk half as much as you listen. Ask open-ended questions, or questions that cannot be answered with a simple yes or no. This method of questioning draws people out and allows you to learn more about them.

Asking questions about the other person is a good way to get them to open up and feel comfortable around you. You'll also make them feel important by showing a genuine interest in what they have to say. Succeed at making the other person feel at ease and important and you are likely to be held in high regard.

4. **Be focused.** You sought a meeting with this person; make sure you are mentally present so that you can recognize and take advantage of opportunities that may open up during the meeting.

5. **Be grateful.** Let the person you're meeting with know how much you appreciate his or her time and advice. A sincere thank you goes a long way when you're attempting to build a relationship. Most people genuinely enjoy helping new grads who show sincere gratitude for such assistance.

6. **Be yourself.** If you pretend to be someone you're not or play a part because you think that is what's expected of you, you deprive the person you're meeting with of knowing the real you. New graduates are particularly susceptible to thinking that they must fit a specific job description or career stereotype. Therefore, when they meet people, they squander valuable time and leave a potential networking contact with a false impression. While

this impression may be favorable, if it is not
authentic it will do nothing to bring the graduate
closer to his or her true career or networking goals.

It's to your advantage to meet with as many different people
as are willing to meet with you. If you connect with someone with whom you have much in common, that's great, but
never pin all of your hopes to one person in your network.
Sometimes even people with the best of intentions make
promises they don't keep. For example, someone might tell
you they'll forward your résumés to someone who has a
job opening. After a few days go by you send an email to
follow up, but receive no response. Eventually, months go
by and still no word. There is no one explanation for why
people make empty promises during networking, but it happens. The best way to prepare for this type of situation is
to meet as many people as possible. Some of these meetings
will blossom into friendships, some into business opportunities, and others into nothing, but with every meeting you
will gain knowledge and experience. And that, in itself, is a
gift.

Who Buys?

If you're meeting face-to-face, the person who does the inviting picks up the check. However, if the invitee insists on
paying, let him. If he then says, "you can get it next time,"
then you know the meeting went well and that you two are

likely to get together again. This also sets the tone for the give-and-take nature of a future relationship. In fact, once you start networking on a regular basis, you will want to start a database of your networking contacts, and keeping track of who paid the last time you met.

The Follow-up

While many meetings occur, very little follow-up seems to take place afterwards. Many people regularly attend networking functions and meetings, but few of them actually succeed in adding people to their network. Simply meeting a person does not give you the right to claim that relationship as part of your network. There is no quick way, nor is there a formula for exactly how long it will take. Building your network is no different than making social friends. Working on the relationship takes time; it takes effort on both sides, but since many people are not as focused on this as you are, more of the effort may be on your shoulders. There's a fine line between reaching out to people and being pushy. Friendships develop at their own pace. If you feel that you are not making progress with someone, or that they do not like you, don't take it personally. Just move on.

A great way to follow up after your first one-on-one meeting with someone you would like to have in your network is to send them a handwritten thank you note. A handwritten note is more memorable than email and therefore has a more powerful impact. The only argument in favor of sending a thank you note via email is immediacy. If you feel that is important in your situation, we advise you to send both. Send your email right away, then drop your handwritten note in the mail a week or so later reiterating that you enjoyed the meeting. You could even include an article that is relevant to the person you met with and mention that you thought they might find the article interesting.

Give First

Building a successful business network requires putting others first. While history reveals many examples of legendary tyrants, there are better ways to do business.

Most people who have reached great success in their career genuinely enjoy the people they work with. They make it a habit of giving of themselves before they ask others to assist them.

> *"If there is any single rule to follow in networking circumstances, it is not 'How can I get the other person to do something for me?' It's 'How can I do something for the other person?'"*
>
> —*Harvey Mackay*

Your goal in any business relationship is to give more than you take. By looking for ways to assist those around you, you cannot help but advance the relationship. Think about the people you encounter on a daily basis. Surely there's someone who is arrogant, selfish, demanding, and rude. Do you look forward to helping that person? Would you go out of your way to let them know information that could be beneficial to them? Of course not. The point is, sooner or later, what goes around comes around. If you are treating people with respect then that, in turn, will enhance your own reputation.

At work, many people place too much weight on the title they hold, even though titles do not command respect; respect must be earned. Similarly, you cannot treat your superiors and peers with respect while being disrespectful to your subordinates. People will not trust you, nor in most cases, like you very much, if you are dismissive of those who are in a supportive role. Many people do a good job of managing up, but it is a special talent to give attention to managing relationship in all directions.

Instead of being the new guy in the networking organization who chimes in with an opinion at every meeting, spend some time listening. Volunteer behind the scenes at events. Take the jobs no one else wants like setting up or working the registration table at an event. If you make it a priority to help other people for a while, when you wish to voice your thoughts or take on a leadership role, people will listen because you will have gained trust and credibility.

As you start attending networking events, look for ways to be helpful to people who are considered influencers. For example, leaders in a member trade association or a volunteer organization get very little support for the heavy lifting or grunt work. Thus, they tend to be grateful to those who are willing to do the less glamorous jobs like calling people to increase attendance at events, or serving on the clean-up committee. This is especially true if you're not clamoring for the public kudos.

"There is no limit to what a man can do or where he can go if he doesn't mind who gets the credit."

—*Raymond Eisenhardt, Sr.*

Remember to Follow Up

Similarly to when you have a one-on-one meeting, when you do meet people at an event that you want to get to know better, send a handwritten note saying how nice it was to meet them. The purpose of your note is to let the other person know that you genuinely enjoyed meeting them. Enclose your business card, even if you gave it to them when you met, because there is a chance that your card never made it back to their office. By enclosing another card you are making it easier for them to remember you, as well as find you in the future.

Thom Says

Since I began my career, I have made it a habit to write between five and ten notes each week. Because so few people take the time to write notes, people often comment on my handwritten notes. It makes it easy for them to start a conversation the next time I see them, or gives them an excuse to send me an email. This starts a dialogue and that leads toward building a relationship.

One year I decided to track how many others did this same thing. I put a shoebox under my desk and placed every note I received in the box after I had read it. By December, not including holiday cards, I had 33 notes in the box, which was less than 10% of the number that I sent out. This solidified my belief that by taking the time to acknowledge people with a note, I would stand out from the crowd.

Networking as a Bank Account

Be careful not to become a drain on the people in your network. Stephen R. Covey's concept of the emotional bank account, which he writes about in his *New York Times* bestseller *The 7 Habits of Highly Effective People,* is equally true in networking. You must build up good will with others before you will have success when you ask them for favors. But, like a bank account, you need to plan your withdrawals carefully to avoid becoming overdrawn. Similar to how a bank regards customers who bounce checks, people frown at those who take more than they give. It's a careful balance. Make it a priority to not become overdrawn with the people you have in your network. If you do find yourself in a situation where you have received a lot of help from an individual, and have not had the opportunity to be of assistance to them, acknowledge the situation and ask if there is anything you can do for them. Thank them. Even if there is nothing you can do to equalize the situation, by simply thanking the other person and acknowledging it, you will have made some headway on clearing the outstanding balance. A sincere thank you is worth a lot.

Turning Networking Contacts into Referrals

While the potential outcomes from networking are as numerous and varied as the reasons people network in the first place, the main objective is always the same: to turn contacts into referrals. A referral occurs when someone informs you of a job opening they are aware of, or introduces you to someone else who knows of one. Generally, these people can also take your résumés straight to the hiring manager, which gives you a huge advantage over everyone else who has to submit their résumés via the company website or job-board.

Anne Says

Sometimes circumstances exist that make it possible for someone to tell you about a job opening, but make it inappropriate for them to hand deliver your résumés. In those situations, the best way to make your résumés stand out from the others is to mail a copy of it, along with your cover letter, to the hiring manager. Here's the secret: Address the letter in your own handwriting. This is a trick direct mail marketing professionals use. Even at work, people can't resist opening a piece of mail that looks like a personal letter.

Leah knows all about the power of a referral because she learned of her job from someone she met in a dance class. After confiding that she was feeling unchallenged at her current job, Leah's new friend suggested she apply for a position at the real estate investment firm where she worked. Leah gave her a résumés and was quickly called in for an interview and hired as an executive assistant. The job had been posted elsewhere, but because a current employee—with a good reputation—referred Leah, her application was fast tracked.

Why are referrals so effective? Simple: People want to work with people they know and like. If a hiring manager knows and likes the employee who is referring you, there's a strong likelihood that the hiring manager will like you too. At any company, when job vacancies need to be filled or new positions are created, there is a better than average chance that the new hire will be someone who was referred. This practice is what creates what is referred to as "the hidden job market."

Jobs that exist, but that may not be posted online or shouted from the rooftops, make up the hidden job market. These jobs are not really secret, they are just more likely to be filled by someone who has an in at that particular company. Most often an "in" means that you know someone who works there, or you have a contact that does. Networking is the single most effective way to learn about openings in the hidden job market and to get a referral that can help you land that job from one of your networking contacts.

Many companies pay employees referral bonuses. Even better than a referral is someone who not only tells you about a job opening and hands your résumés to human resources, but who also puts in a good word for you. If that happens, then you have turned that referral into a recommendation. When Matt needed to find a new position, a former colleague who knew of a position gave him a great recommendation. Again, because he knew someone with an inside contact, Matt's application was put on the fast track and he got the job of director of technology for a non-profit in Illinois.

As you build your career, your managers will play a large role in your future employment prospects because they will be your professional references—they are the people who can personally vouch for the quality of your work. If you don't have much work experience, or any at all, volunteering for committees within prominent networking organizations is a great way to build a list of references. For example, let's say you want to pursue a career in marketing, but you don't have any marketing experience. Join an organization like the American Marketing Association and volunteer to be on one or several committees. Now you'll have prominent marketing professionals from your own community who can vouch for the quality of work you produce related to marketing.

Keep in mind that the secret to successful networking is to approach relationships with a give-and-take mentality. Just like your personal friendships, successful professional relationships are built upon mutual respect and trust. Avoid having a self-centered mindset, and look for ways to nurture your new friendships by keeping your eyes and ears open for opportunities that would benefit your growing list of networking contacts. Make this second nature and you'll be well on your way to establishing yourself as someone people are lining up to get to know better.

Take Aways

Put as much effort into developing your professional relationships as you do your personal friendships.

Treat everyone with respect.

People want to help people they know and like by giving them referrals, recommendations, and references.

5

THE POWER TOOLS:

FOR EVERY YOUNG PROFESSIONAL

Most of your success in networking will depend on your ability to master the intangible art of relationship building. A critical part of building relationships is knowing how to make a good first impression. To make a good first impression you need to have a professional appearance and be approachable. In addition, you must give careful consideration to the condition and presentation of the materials that you carry with you—such as business cards. These items are an extension of your personal brand and they, too, play a role in helping to enhance or detract from a first impression.

How to Make a Good First Impression

Right or not, the moral message of *don't judge a book by its cover* gets lost in the hustle and bustle that is networking. The people you want to network with will decide whether or not you're worth their time based on your appearance and perhaps, if they're feeling generous, the first few words that come out of your mouth. You'll have an easier time at networking events if you simply accept this fact and do your best to make a favorable first impression.

Appearance

As far as your appearance is concerned, whether consciously or subconsciously, there are four things that people notice about you right away: your clothes, your hair, your hands, and your scent, if it's strong. While this last point may seem laughable, you'd be surprised at how often a potent scent kills a possible success story. Just consider:

Chili Dogma

"Rex" headed to his university career fair full of hope and armed with more than a hundred résumés printed on premium grade stationery. He had a goal of talking to at least 50 companies. When he arrived he was disappointed to find there were only about 35 companies in attendance, but he set out to talk to every recruiter that was offering a salaried entry-level position.

The morning session went great, and afterwards he approached the companies he was least interested in. This gave him the opportunity to practice his introduction and get more comfortable with the on-the-spot interviews that some companies were doing. The recruiters that he spoke with seemed genuinely interested in him and a few even indicated that an on-campus interview would be forthcoming. Rex was elated.

When the lunch break arrived, he hustled over to the school cafeteria, wolfed down a chili-cheese dog loaded with onions and mustard, then hurried back into the gymnasium to speak with his top company picks. To his surprise, the afternoon session went lousy. Recruiters didn't seem to want to talk to him for more than 30 seconds. He barely had enough time to finish his introduction before the recruiter would take his résumés, lay it on a pile, and offer the obligatory, "Thanks for stopping by."

Rex decided to leave early and was heading toward the exit when someone called out to him. Rex turned around and saw one of the first recruiters he'd talked to that morning. "Rex, you made a great impression on me this morning so I want to help you out. I heard one of the other recruiters talking after lunch, and, well, here." He pulled a pack of Tic Tacs out of his suit pocket. Rex was horrified, but after a few minutes he laughed and thanked the thoughtful recruiter for letting him know that it wasn't his résumés that was offending the other company representatives ... it was bad breath!

Aside from onions, we advise you to avoid cigarettes, heavy perfume or cologne, and any other strong smells that someone might find offensive. Anne once knew a pregnant HR manager who had to conduct several interviews during her first trimester when she was especially sensitive to odors. Several job candidates had their interviews cut short because they were literally causing this poor woman to become nauseous. Why take a chance of losing out on a job, a sale, or acquiring a new client?

Clothes are arguably the most important aspect of your appearance when networking. If you look shabby, people will assume you don't take yourself seriously, and thus, they won't take you seriously either. Don't make the mistake of tricking yourself into believing that people won't notice those wrinkles or the two-day-old coffee stain on your cuff. They will. For young professionals, the most important article of clothing is the *suit*. Every young professional needs to have at least one good suit in their wardrobe. Chicago stylist Erin Carpenter offers these tips for new graduates:

When shopping for a new suit, invest in the best quality you can afford, without going over the top in head-to-toe Armani. It's better to have a single well-fitting suit in a classic color than a few cheaply made ones.

Choose wool or wool blends over synthetics. Dark grey, navy, or black are best, though tan or brown are also acceptable. Don't expect a suit to fit you perfectly off the rack—factor the cost of professional alterations into your budget to achieve a perfect fit; it's worth it! (Some stores offer free alterations with purchase, so be sure to ask, and shop with enough time to allow for them.)

When you get dressed, make sure your suit is clean and pressed and that pants are creased if and where they should be. Wear a lightly starched, collared, long sleeve dress shirt in bright white (no dinginess, stains, or ring around the collar!), and allow the cuffs to peek out under your sleeves about a half inch. If your shirt calls for cufflinks, keep them understated. If you wear a watch, make it a basic silver- or gold-toned one and leave the snazzy one you received as a graduation gift at home.

In addition, here are a few gender-specific guidelines for how to wear your new suit:

Men

- Suit should be 2-3 button, single-breasted—Skip the pin-striped version; in some industries it's too formal.
- Shirts should be buttoned to the top.
- Undershirts should be worn, and should be white.

- Tie should be silk and in a solid color or small pattern—nothing too loud, cartooned, or tied in a bow.

- Shoes should be lace-up leather, preferably in black.

- Shoes should be very clean, shined and cobbled if need be—worn heels and soles indicate you don't care.

- Socks should match your shoes and be long enough to cover your leg when you sit down.

- Belt should be leather, match the shoes, and should not have a phone clipped to it.

- Pockets shouldn't carry more than necessary, and jangling coins should be left behind.

- A watch and wedding ring (if you're married) are the only pieces of jewelry you should wear.

Women

- Consider a skirt suit. It may sound archaic, but in many industries, pantsuits are considered inappropriate for female job candidates. If you can only afford one good suit, this is your best bet.

- Skirts may be A-line or pencil style, and should reach the middle of the knee.

- Jackets should be 1-2 button, single-breasted.

- Blouses should be buttoned to a conservative height.

- Bras should be nude, smooth, and out of sight.

- Ears should showcase only one set of small earrings.

- Other jewelry should be minimal: a simple necklace and one ring per hand, max. Skip noisy bracelets.

- Legs should never be bare. They may not be the most fashion-forward choice, but sheer nude (but not "suntan") or black hose are most appropriate when your goal is to make a good first impression.

- Shoes should be closed toed and moderately heeled—stilettos are inappropriate.

- Only one item should be carried: a leather portfolio or classic leather tote-style bag to carry materials relevant to the event you're attending. It should also serve as your handbag.

While a personal style is good, make sure that your appearance fits within the standards for industry. As with so many things, knowing your audience is imperative. If you, as a man, will be attending an event where most people will be coming straight from the office, you will be out of place in a casual pair of pants and a golf shirt. It's smarter to be better dressed. Slacks are a better choice than khakis. In addition, even if others are wearing polo-style shirts, a crisp dress shirt is a better choice. For women, while a pantsuit is appropriate at almost every networking event, if in doubt wear your skirt suit. In addition, there are countless articles, blogs, books, and image consultants who can assist you in making the correct wardrobe choices for any particular event or occasion if you're still unsure. Better department stores offer free personal shopping services.

Your hair should be styled appropriately for your age and profession. And since you will be shaking hands often, your hands should be clean, and your nails neatly manicured.

Approachability

If you look approachable, people will walk right up to you and start a conversation. This makes networking much easier for you if you're not always the one who has to come up with a clever opener. To help improve your approachability factor, here are three things to keep in mind when you're meeting people for the first time:

Smile. A genuine smile puts people at ease and shows that you are open to conversation and meeting new people. If you're shy, a great trick is to pretend that everyone in the room is one of your best friends whom you haven't seen in awhile. Thinking of something or someone pleasant actually makes us smile! Don't just reserve a smile for when you're being introduced to someone either. Smile as you pass people in the halls, at the buffet table, and at the coat rack. Seeming friendly never goes amiss.

The firm handshake. In the United States it is customary to shake someone's hand when you meet them. Unless you are a famous germaphobe, like Donald Trump, most people will expect a handshake. A handshake can express confidence or a lack thereof.

Eye contact. Making and then maintaining eye contact with the person you are talking to is critical. By looking someone in the eyes you are showing them that you are interested in what they have to say. You are also showing them that you are fully present in the conversation. Some people say that looking people in the eyes also conveys honesty.

Never Confuse Visibility with Credibility

Networking can take place anytime and anywhere, and it's especially likely to happen spontaneously when you're motivated to get started. It's important for the recent grad to get out there and be seen within the professional community. If you're already working, start networking within your own company, online, at your local coffee shop, on the train en route to work, or at the gym. If you are still looking for a job, remember that any place you go becomes a networking venue if you have the proper mindset.

Some people who are new to networking get so caught up with the idea of "being seen" that they lose sight of why they started networking in the first place. Instead of being seen as someone that other people want to get to know, these novice networkers are viewed as selfish networkers. This happens for a number of reasons, but most commonly because they go into a networking situation so focused on themselves that they don't pay enough attention to those they're trying to meet.

Treat Everyone with Respect

We all get caught up in our own stuff. This can make it easy to forget about others' feelings. Once you've been working for a few years you'll be amazed by how often people will cancel a meeting at the last minute by saying that "something suddenly came up." Translation: Something more important than *you* has come up.

Here are a few basic common courtesy tips that should become second nature to you if they're not already:

- Use the words "please" and "thank you" frequently.
- Arrive at appointments on time or better yet, early.
- Call if you're running late.
- Ignore your cell phone or even better, turn it off.
- Do what you say you're going to do.
- Apologize if you screw up.

We also want to make you aware of something very disrespectful that occurs alarmingly often at networking events. More times than not, people who are engaged in one conversation are scanning the room to see who else is present. Once they spot that "better" person, they abruptly end the conversation and rush off to talk to that other individual. While it's important to circulate and talk to as many people as possible, how you conduct yourself in the present is part of the impression you will leave behind. Focus on the person you're speaking to.

If you want to end a conversation, there are several polite ways to do it. Acknowledge the other person's comments and tell them that you look forward to talking with them more in the future. Another strategy is to tell the other person that you do not want to monopolize all of their time at the event, as you know there are many others that they want to speak with. You have put the focus on them. Over time you will get better at this. After all, learning how to end conversations gracefully truly is an art.

Thom Says

Although "Darrin" and I had mutual friends, whenever our paths crossed he was less than cordial. Then I began working for a law firm and Darrin, whose business offering was consulting services to law firms, suddenly wanted to get to know me. More amazing was that when I first met him, my primary clients were partners in law firms. By the time my value was obvious to Darrin, I had already established a negative opinion of him and would not have recommended him under any circumstance.

Memory Tricks

Have you ever run into someone you have not seen in a long time and they ask you specific things, such as if you had fun on your recent birthday, if your dog is doing okay, or if you've been back to your favorite restaurant recently? It's impressive when people remember the details of your life and it sends a clear message that they were listening to you the previous time you met. The more you know about a person, the easier it is to build a connection.

Taking a genuine interest in people makes you a more effective networker. Recalling the details of someone's past experiences, their interests, their careers and their families will help you stand out from the crowd. Unfortunately, this won't happen on its own; you need to make an effort to gather information about people and find a way to track and easily recall it.

When you are actively meeting new people, on occasion you will have trouble remembering their names. To avoid this, learn some memory tricks. Here are a few basic tips to get you started:

Repeat the person's name out loud or introduce them to someone else. Using their name in conversation may help you recall their name later. You can also invent a relationship in your mind between their name and their physical characteristics. One example for Shirley Temple could be "her curly (rhymes with Shirley) hair is cut short near her temples."

Always get a business card. Rather than just taking the card and putting it in your pocket or bag, look at the card and then make a positive comment about it to the person who has just handed it to you. This will help you commit this person to memory, and it's a respectful thing to do.

Add people to your database. Regardless of which kind of system you use to keep track of your contacts, be sure to regularly add new people into your database.

Anne's System

After entering the contact information from the card into my electronic database, I tape my cards in a notebook and make notes on the page to help me remember specific things we talked about. Then, I review this information when I'm likely to run into the person again, or when I'm looking to make referrals.

Carol, a popular business speaker, avoids saying "nice to meet you" when she is introduced to people. Over the years Carol has met thousands of people at events where she has spoken and, since she was the expert, these people all remember her. Often "nice to meet you" is met with "oh, we have met before...." Carol has found that "nice to see you" works better. However, if you are introduced to someone who obviously knows you, and you have not the foggiest idea of who they are, it is best to own up to it and admit that you do not remember them. If you handle it with poise and sincerity, it's a lot better than pretending you know them.

Invest in Developing Public Speaking Skills

Public speaking is often cited as the number one thing most feared by Americans. Death ranks number two. If this rings a bell, we have two words for you: Toastmasters International.

Thom has been an active member of Toastmasters for two decades and is still amazed by how many people have never heard of the organization, which has been around since 1924. Its charter reads: "Through participation in the Toastmasters Communication and Leadership Program, people from all backgrounds learn to effectively speak, conduct a meeting, manage a department or business, lead, delegate, and motivate." These are all skills that can help you in business.

There are Toastmasters clubs in every major US metropolitan area and in 80 countries. Many people who are familiar with the organization have never looked into it because they think the clubs are made up of only advanced speakers. In fact, clubs are made up of people with a variety of speaking skills, and you will benefit from enhancing your public speaking skills, regardless of your industry or job function.

In addition, many people have actually made business connections from people they have met within Toastmasters. People have met future employers and employees because they are exposed to people who are focused on personal growth, and often find like-minded others. Thom met Chad Goldwasser, co-author of *Some Assembly Required: A Networking Guide for Real Estate,* in his Toastmasters Club. Eight years later they wrote the book together.

More information about Toastmasters is available at *www.toastmasters.org.*

Tools of the Trade

Personal branding is not only for the Internet. In the offline world, the materials you carry around with you to assist you in your networking efforts are a huge part of how you are perceived. These are the tools of the networking trade! Think of your business card as an extension of yourself. For example, you wouldn't show up to an event in dirty or wrinkled clothes would you? Well, neither should you hand someone a business card that's been torn. In this section we'll discuss some important things to keep in mind about the materials you carry when you're meeting people for the first time.

Business Cards

Your business card is your single most important networking tool. Once you have met someone and decided that you want to get to know them better, you need to get their business card so that you can easily access their pertinent information. Carry your own cards with you at all times. To prevent your cards from becoming beat up, keep them in a case. If you have one with your alma mater on the cover, use it. This is a great invitation for others who went to your school to strike up a conversation. Many universities sell or give away business card holders to alumni because they want you to continue making connections with fellow alums after you've left campus. Of course, they don't mind the free advertising either. Contact your alumni relations office to find out if they offer business card holders.

You may be surprised about where a business card can come in handy. Steve, a financial planner, exchanged business cards with someone he met in his local hospital's emergency room, where they were both waiting to be seen. This exchange turned into new business. If you are not yet working, have business cards made. Some universities even have templates you can use with your school's logo. If not, tasteful use of color can be just as appealing. Here are a few pointers for you:

Have a professional look to your cards. While you can purchase inexpensive cards online or print them on your laser printer, if you go cheap, you will look cheap. The card is part of your image. Card stock is a must.

Print lots of them. Cards, even high-quality cards, are relatively inexpensive.

Enclose business cards in your correspondence. Of course there does come a point where you can overdo this, so use your best judgment. Early in his career Thom had a prospective client tell him that, after a year of receiving marketing materials from him, she had collected a whole box of his cards. While she said this jokingly, he got the message.

Use a color logo on your card. Be sure your email address is on your card. For those graduates still looking for work, be sure to use an appropriate email address.

Be brief. Your business card is not your résumés or a marketing brochure. If you do a good job of networking and making connections, your name and company should be enough to trigger a reminder about what you discussed when you met.

Go with the standard business card size and shape.
Unusually shaped cards are difficult to place in a wallet or card case, and thus might not make it back to the recipient's office, which means your contact information is lost.

Have a light color or even white on the reverse side of your card. While color is good, you want to be sure that people can jot notes on it if they wish.

Nametags

When attending a networking event, knowing someone's first name and the company they work for is an easy conversation opener. A conversation can easily begin with "Hi Jim, I know someone who works for Bank of America …" or "Tanya, I have not heard of Image Base. What does your company do?" Many times people either do not wear nametags (or, frighteningly, the organization hosting the event does not provide them) or the text is too small for the average person to read. The most common mistake of all occurs when people have to write their own nametag: it's illegible. People with less than perfect penmanship need to make sure that it's clear and it's neat. Be sure to put your first and last name and, under that, your company name. Some people shy away from writing the company name or they put it in code. The law firm Andrews Kurth is referred to internally as AK. If an attorney writes "AK" on his or her nametag at a public event, people will not understand. However, when a company is branded by its initials—IBM and 3M are good examples of this—it is not only acceptable, it is preferred. One final point about nametags: wear them where they can be seen. This does not mean on your belt or in another obscure but visible location. Nametags make it easy for others to learn your name and your company affiliation. Let your nametag do its job.

Stationery

High-quality, personalized note cards are worth the investment. We both have some very nice fold-over cards with our names printed on the front. No matter how much companies try to believe that customers have relationships with the business, the truth is that the relationship rests with the individuals who represent the business. Finally, always write in pen. It's hard to take a letter written in pencil seriously, no matter how thoughtfully it's written.

Leave the Baggage at Home

At a networking event, in a roomful of people you are probably meeting for the first time, the last thing you need is to be weighed down by a large purse or briefcase. Be sure you can maneuver easily and not get stuck fumbling around with straps and pockets when someone is trying to converse with you. Bring a lightweight, professional-looking bag and plan out ahead of time where you'll put the business cards you receive. Make sure you store your cards (and résumés if appropriate) in an easy-to-reach place and bring plenty. Having a place for everything and being able to access what you need swiftly makes you look organized and will make you feel more confident.

Follow-up Etiquette

Beyond making initial contact by sending a short note, if the person is someone you want to get to know better then you need to plan for further follow-up. The trick here is to not be too pushy. If you force it by sending a note and then immediately calling to schedule coffee or lunch, the other person may feel uncomfortable, especially if they did not feel the same about you. If you are active in the organization that hosted the event where you met, it's likely that you will cross paths with people fairly regularly. This gives you the opportunity to talk a few times, and then suggest that you get together for coffee. If the person agrees, scheduling the next meeting is very easy. If the person does not jump at the opportunity, don't press the issue, just continue to talk with them as your paths cross. Some people are not as aggressive as others in their efforts to grow their network, and others do not like to do so at all. Become good at reading other people.

When you do meet with someone for coffee or lunch, keep it casual. Save elaborate meals for special contacts or clients, and instead go to your local coffee house or casual lunch spot. Let the other person pick the place if possible. Even if you do the inviting and plan to pay, when you agree on a date and time ask, "Where would be a convenient place for you?" If someone has to drive across town to meet with you, you run a greater risk of their canceling than if you meet at the restaurant next to their office. Some people try to invite new contacts to outings or venues that require a large time investment. Generally, people are not willing to set aside four hours or more for someone when there is no mutually beneficial established connection. To slot someone into a "bigger" event before you know them well enough could cause them to refuse the invitation, and limit your chance to advance the friendship.

As networking becomes part of your routine, you will meet all kinds of people. Some you will like, others you won't, and a few won't like you. Don't take it personally. In networking, as in life, not everyone gets along all the time. Accept this fact and move on when you encounter someone that is not receptive to building a relationship. By doing so you will free up more time for the people who do want to get to know you.

Take Aways

Knowing how to make a good first impression when you're networking is vital to your success.

Being viewed as approachable can help make you more successful at networking.

Your physical personal branding materials should look professional and be easily accessible at events.

6

EVENTS AND ORGANIZATIONS:

GET AHEAD BY GETTING INVOLVED

Becoming an active member of a few relevant organizations that attract like-minded individuals is a must for any new graduate looking to build their network. In other words, if you want to get ahead, look for ways to get involved. Networking groups such as community-based organizations, professional associations, and alumni clubs are good places to start.

Getting involved puts you in the path of people who have already established themselves as business leaders. Getting to know these more experienced professionals is a smart career move for several reasons. Not only do employers seek job candidates who feel comfortable around executives, but also these local leaders already have large networks and are often considered to be *influencers* within a specific field, industry, or community. Because others respect them and trust their judgment, these people can influence your career by giving you their stamp of approval. To be blunt: they can help you get a job faster than your campus career center.

You'll also save time by joining organizations. Attending events will bring you in contact with many people at once, all of whom you may have future one-on-one meetings with in order to develop a more solid relationship. Think about it: within the span of just an hour or two, you can meet dozens of people that have the potential to become an important part of your professional or personal life.

Choosing the Right Organizations

Regardless of where you live and what you do (or *want* to do), there are a number of organizations you can join that can help you attain your networking goals. In order to find out about these groups though, you'll have to do some sleuthing; these groups aren't going to come knocking on your door as soon as you graduate. So, how can you find these organizations?

1. **Search the web, your local newspapers, and business publications.** Most of these organizations have websites that list membership criteria and mission statements. You should be able to find the types of organizations you're looking for by typing in a few keywords in addition to your city name. Don't neglect your local publications, either, as they often list the events being hosted by local organizations.

2. **Ask peers, professors, and professional friends.** Find out which organizations are highly regarded by the business people in the community. Even if your friends don't work in the same industry or city as you, they're worth asking because they may know someone who can point you in the right direction.

3. **Attend local events and ask people there.** Anytime you find yourself at an event in the community, ask the people you meet if they know of any organizations for young professionals in your field.

Once you have a list of some organizations that interest you, you'll need to do some more research to make sure you join only the groups that will be the right fit for you. Membership, like networking, is a two-way street. You must be able to contribute *to* the organization, as well as benefit *from* it.

Ask yourself:

1. What do I hope to gain from joining this association?

2. What do I hope to bring to this group?

3. Is this organization the best use of my time and energy?

4. Will this group help me achieve my networking goals?

5. Do I agree with the mission and the values of this organization?

Now let's take a look at a few types of organizations to consider getting involved in.

Professional Associations

Professional associations are usually non-profits that focus their membership around a particular industry, such as healthcare or education, or job function, such as accountants or lawyers. These groups range in size from small, local organizations, to huge international associations. Many national associations have local or regional chapters. Members benefit not only from networking with local peers, but also by accessing the resources of a nationwide community as well. National associations often have annual conferences and live online meetings or webinars where members can meet like-minded professionals from different parts of the country and learn from their experiences. The American Marketing Association and the American Society of Civil Engineers are examples of professional associations with a widespread national presence.

Community-Based Organizations

There are several different kinds of community-based organizations that provide local opportunities to network with people who have similar interests. Here are four you're likely to find in your own neighborhood:

1. **Social clubs.** Singles groups, sports clubs, and groups for people with common interests, such as dance, gardening, and pets, are a popular

networking venue for recent graduates. The Chicago Sports and Social Club is an example of one such club.

2. **Volunteer organizations.** Many cities have formal or informal groups that give their time to help improve the community in some way. Sometimes these groups focus on raising money for, or donating time to, local charities. Other groups focus on community beautification projects, building houses for the less fortunate, or providing resources for local non-profits. The Taproot Foundation, for example, recruits volunteers with experience in marketing, HR, IT, or strategy management to perform pro bono services for non-profits in six major US cities. And Habitat for Humanity, of course, is an example of an international volunteer organization that offers volunteer opportunities at the local level. For most of these volunteer groups there is no official membership roster or requirement: You simply sign up and volunteer for projects that last anywhere from a day to several months.

3. **Service organizations.** These groups do tend to have membership requirements and primarily focus on humanitarian and environmental issues. Lions Clubs International is an example of an international

service organization with local chapters in almost every US city.

4. **Special interest groups.** These are less formal clubs and groups built around a common interest like sports, books, politics, favorite TV shows, or a specific profession. They tend to pop into existence suddenly and disappear more quickly than social clubs because their sustainability is wholly dependent on the people who start them. Despite their short run times, they can be a great place to start building a network. In Anne's neighborhood for example, there is a foodie special interest group that meets at a local restaurant each week to talk about favorite foods, wines, and sometimes watch episodes of "Top Chef."

There are several other types of organizations you can get involved with in your community as well—church groups, charities, and community centers just to name a few. The only rule you must adhere to if you want to become a successful networker is to genuinely be interested in the group you join or volunteer your time to. If you just show up to schmooze, but are not honestly committed to the mission statement of the organization, you will not succeed in building genuine and lasting relationships. People always see through a façade. A great website to visit if you're unsure where to start your search for a community-based organization is *www.volunteermatch.com*. This website helps would-be volunteers clarify their interests and skills, and then matches them with a local organization in need of assistance. You can also visit *www.meetup.com* and search by zip code and topic of interest to see what groups are meeting up in your neighborhood.

University Alumni Organizations

If you do not already belong to your alma mater's alumni association, put this book down, go straight to your computer, get online and find out how you can join, now. Alumni groups usually have quarterly or monthly events where you can meet people with whom you already have at least one thing in common—your alma mater. Alumni want to help other alumni. They are happy to make introductions, help fellow alums get acclimated to a new community, find local resources, serve as mentors, or even find jobs.

If you were a member of a sorority or fraternity in college, you're in luck. The bonds of brotherhood and sisterhood stay strong long after graduation, and individual sororities and fraternities have their own national alumni organizations you can join. In addition, many colleges and universities now have formal Greek system alumni associations that host events and have their own member directories. The easiest way to find out about becoming a member of these organizations is to do a simple Google search, or call your university's alumni relations office.

My involvement in the alumni club gives me an opportunity to find ways to offer value to others, not just look for quick results for myself. As I get to know someone and learn about their professional and personal interests, I am always on the lookout for helpful studies, articles, and contacts that I can share with them. Not only have I furthered my relationship with my network in this way, I have become a go-to resource for information for them. This has led to professional opportunities and leads for me as well.

*Bo Sandine, President
Kellogg School of Management
Alumni Club of Orange County*

Membership Organizations

Elks
www.elks.org

Lions
www.lionsclubs.org

Rotary International
www.rotary.org

Toastmasters International
www.toastmasters.org

Kiwanis International
www.kiwanis.org

Women's Organizations

85 Broads
www.85broads.com
This global professional network was founded by women who worked for Goldman Sachs at 85 Broad Street, the investment banking firm's New York City headquarters. They have a large presence on college and graduate school campuses as well.

Business and Professional Women
www.bpwusa.org
This group promotes equity for women in the workplace through advocacy and education.

National Association of Women Business Owners (NAWBO)
www.nawbo.org
You do not need to be a business owner to join this networking group, which hosts monthly events and a national conference each year.

The Association of Junior Leagues International
www.ajli.org
There are Junior Leagues in almost every city in the US and in many foreign countries. Its emphasis is on leader-

ship training, volunteer management, and developing the business skills you need to be successful.

Professional Associations

American Accounting Association
www.aaahq.org

American Bar Association
www.abanet.org

National Human Resources Association
www.humanresources.org

National Society of Professional Engineers

www.nspe.org

Public Relations Society of America
www.prsa.org

The American Marketing Association
www.marketingpower.com

The Professional Association for Design (AIGA
www.aiga.org

Leveraging Your Involvement

So now that you've joined one or two networking organizations (in addition to your alumni association!), what's next? It's not enough to pay the membership dues and slap the name of the organization on your résumés. To truly belong to the group and to make the most of your membership in any organization, you have to actually participate on a regular basis. Here are some ways to get the most out of your involvement within any organization.

Learn the History

Every organization has a story and vision around which members rally. It's in your best interest to be knowledgeable about the organization to which you belong. Why was it founded? How long has it been in existence? What are some of the major benefits of membership? What types of people are drawn to the group? Are there any famous or important members of interest? Knowing about the group of people you are surrounding yourself with is an important aspect of maintaining your credibility.

Use the Membership Resources

Most membership organizations seek to promote the interests of its members through various events, educational programs, and all sorts of shared resources. Your membership dues and event fees allow these types of resources to be made available. These will vary from group to group, but usually include at least some of the following:

> **Membership database.** Most organizations have an online database (or print directory) with members' job titles, company names, and contact information. It's a

good idea to familiarize yourself with who your fellow members are so that you can identify people you want to seek out at future events. Do not email people you don't know and ask for favors just because you belong to the same organization. This is a quick way to earn yourself the reputation of a selfish networker.

Seminars and conferences. Most organizations hold at least one annual conference and several regional or local seminars throughout the year. Any time you have the opportunity to be in the same room as people in the same or similar profession to yours, you should find a way to be there. Once you're there, make the effort to meet as many people as you can. Be sure to get a copy of the attendee list before you leave, as not all attendees will be members. This way you can reach out to people afterwards if for some reason you weren't able to exchange contact information when you met.

Discounts. Some organizations offer member discounts at local businesses or for events of all kinds. Be sure to check out the group's website or membership package so you can take advantage of any discounts.

Newsletters and publications. Reading the newsletter (and other publications produced by the organization) is a great way to stay informed about the organization's benefits, members, and activities. The newsletter is also a starting point for anyone who wants to establish credibility within a particular field or industry by writing articles. Organizations are always looking for original content.

Be Visible

In order to get ahead, people must be able to picture you in a leadership role. Organizations and associations are always in need of volunteer leaders, the people who can step up and do the work that's required to keep the group operating smoothly. Dig in and join a committee or offer to run an event. This is your chance to prove you can take a project and run with it. And, as a bonus, these types of projects are great résumés builders too!

Volunteer for Tedious Tasks

Everyone wants to be seen as a leader and as someone that handles responsibility and authority gracefully. But the truth is that many networking organizations have too many leaders and not enough actual members to do the heavy lifting. As a newcomer, you can quickly make a good impression and establish yourself as a dependable member by volunteering for the committees and tasks that make others cringe. Not only will you win their gratitude, you'll be perceived as someone who is not afraid to roll up their sleeves and get the job done. This is a trait of a true leader.

Build Relationships, Not a Contact List

If most of the people you meet at events form a positive impression of you, that's a great first step. But until you follow up and develop those contacts into relationships, you are merely filling your contact database with names and email addresses. Focus on building trust with a few key individuals within prominent organizations. This is especially true when you're meeting new people through online social networks. (See Chapter 8 for best practices in building relationships through social networks.)

Don't Overextend Yourself

It's one thing to want to pull your weight, but it's something else entirely to exaggerate what you can realistically contribute. Be careful not to make promises you can't keep, such as agreeing to recruit more people than you actually know to attend an upcoming event. It's easy to fall into the trap of wanting to please people, but making commitments and not following through is a major networking error that will damage your reputation within any organization.

On the other hand, even if you can come through on all the promises you make, be careful not to over commit yourself. Networking should be an enjoyable supplemental activity to your regular job. Be careful not to let it become a whole other profession in itself. You don't want to burn yourself out by trying to be in too many places at once.

Know When to Say When

As your career evolves, your networking needs and goals will too. Not every organization is going to suit you for the entire length of your career, and that's okay. While it's hard to move on from an organization that has enhanced your life, you need to focus your networking efforts where you'll get the most bang for your buck. You can't belong to many associations and clubs and expect to be an effective member of each group. Know your limits. Renew your memberships only in the organizations in which you intend to maintain an active role.

Making the Most of Events

Just like joining organizations, be selective about the events you attend. Each event is only worth your effort if you go into it with a networking plan in mind. Every time you consider going to an event, ask yourself what your goal in attending that event is. The more concrete your answer, the more probable it is that you will be successful.

If you are unclear why you're going to a specific event, not really sure what you stand to gain from attending, or if your heart just simply isn't in it, your time is better spent else-where. Too many people halfheartedly make their way to events, show up late, sit by themselves, speak to no one, and then leave early. These people go home cranky, thinking it was a total waste of their time, when it was actually a wasted opportunity.

Here are several strategies you can fold into your strategic networking plans to ensure that the events you attend are a good investment for you:

Research the event or host organization prior to attending. The Internet makes this a snap. Before you commit to attending an event, do some research about the host organization and the event itself. Look for comments from past attendees. If your research yields positive results you can head to the event ready to engage in conversation. If you find more people have a negative perception of the organization or event, you can skip it altogether.

Attend with a buddy. Recruiting a friend or colleague to go with you has several advantages, not the least of which is that you are not on your own. For networking novices or introverts, it can be soothing to know that someone else is there with you. Your buddy can give you a safe landing point if you find yourself wandering alone through the crowd or between conversations. If you're more of a natural networker, attending with a buddy provides the opportunity to meet and learn about twice as many people if you split up and then introduce each other to your new contacts.

Arrive early. The best networking actually happens at the beginning of an event. It's something more experienced networkers use to their advantage. Whether the event is in the morning, afternoon, or evening, the action happens before the actual program even begins. Here's why:

At the end of an event, people are in a rush to get back to work, home, out for drinks, or to the gym. Since many events include a speaker or other type of program, the actual networking time is limited. If you want to interact with the other attendees, your best bet is to arrive early, especially if there is someone in particular you want to connect with.

In addition, by arriving early you can scope out the registration table and scan the pre-printed nametags to find out who else is going to be there. Then you can strategically pick and choose whom you want to meet. Of course, it's also much easier to walk into an empty room than it is to try and join 300 people already engaged in conversation. When you arrive first, it's like being the host of the party instead of an out-of-town guest.

Spend time initiating new relationships and building existing ones. We're all guilty of spending an entire event catching up with a friend, former colleague, or someone else we know. Although this happens, be careful not to let it become a habit. While it's important to maintain your current relationships, you must also commit to meeting new people and initiating new relationships, even though this is more intimidating. Aim to meet at least five new people at each event you attend. If you keep this goal in mind while you're circulating, you will be conscious of not spending too much time with any one person. Of course, be careful not to start scanning the room once you've decided your time is up with the person to whom you're currently speaking. You want to meet new people, but not at the expense of offending anyone.

Sit strategically. At networking events, people tend to sit near people they already know. This is a mistake because ultimately you squander an opportunity to get to know someone new. Even though it's more comfortable to chat with someone you already know, it's not the best use of your networking time. The next time you attend an event, make an effort to sit next to someone you'd like to meet instead of someone with whom you already have an established rapport.

Follow up within three days of the event. Follow-up is the most neglected aspect of networking, despite the fact that it also happens to be the most important. It usually goes something like this:

You meet someone at an event and have a great conversation. You go home excited to meet up with this person for coffee or lunch. A few days go by before you have a chance to sit down and send an email or note. Just as you turn on your computer, or get out your personalized stationery, you realize that you misplaced their business card. Argh! Don't let this happen to you. Instead, as soon as you get home, enter their contact information into your own personal filing system. Write a note, or draft an email and make sure to send either one (or both) within three days. Prompt follow-up can make or break a new relationship. Make it a priority and a habit.

Event Etiquette

At each event you attend, you want to come across as professional, polished, and personable, not to mention competent and confident. Knowing the proper etiquette will help you make this impression. So, if you aren't familiar with the etiquette involved in attending events, this next section is just for you because it's important that you know how to conduct yourself in social networking situations.

Know how to make introductions. The most common networking gaffe involves introductions. Either people forget or neglect to introduce themselves or the people they're with. In order to avoid creating an awkward moment, practice making introductions.

Let's say it's your first time attending an event hosted by the professional association you've just joined. You walk into the room and realize that you don't know a single person in there. However, you notice a rather approachable looking group of people so you wander over to where they are chatting amongst themselves and then you freeze. Now you are just standing there and, if you're an introvert, chances are you're not really listening to the conversation because you're feeling self-conscious. If you're more of a natural networker, you've probably caught the gist, and are waiting for a lull in the conversation before introducing yourself.

The proper thing to do is to nod to the group as you approach. Try to make eye contact with everyone. This lets people know you're coming to join in, but signals that you're not going to interrupt their conversation. Now, if the people in the group know their etiquette, they will pause and introduce themselves and give you a chance to introduce yourself. If they don't, you may have to wait until there is a natural pause before introducing yourself. Either way, an example of a good introduction for this type of situation is:

"Hi everyone, I'm Gabby Morley. I'm a web developer for Purple Monkey Studios and I'm a new member of this association. This is actually my first event, and I'm really excited to meet everyone and learn more about this group."

If one of those people knew you, proper etiquette would be for them to take the initiative and introduce you to the group. But when you are new to networking organizations, especially at the beginning of your career, and particularly if you're in a new city, chances are you'll be on your own the first few times.

When introducing others, there are a few additional rules to keep in mind. First, it's considered proper etiquette to introduce the person with less experience to a more senior professional. For example:

"Kelly, I'd like you to meet Chris Kroll, Managing Director of Oak Tree Bank. Chris, this is Kelly Davis, a freelance graphic designer I've worked with on several corporate projects."

Respect quiet time. When you're attending events that include an educational program or feature a speaker, the time comes to stop talking and listen to the speaker, no matter how engrossed you are in a particular conversation. Respect the host and the speaker by paying attention. If one of your colleagues, friends, or new contacts attempts to engage you in conversation at an inappropriate time, smile, nod and then break eye contact, returning your attention to the focus of the event. If the person persists, you may have to tell him or her (politely and quietly) that you would like to listen to the speaker. Respectful behavior is always noticed and appreciated. Keep in mind that disrespectful behavior is always noticed too.

Silence your cell phone or PDA. While these devices have done a lot to make networking easier and more convenient, they have also created some etiquette challenges. Simply put, unless you are someone on whom the balance of life and death depends, there is no acceptable time to answer a call, read, or return a text. By doing so you tell everyone you're with that they are not as important as you think you are. In addition, when more senior professionals catch junior employees fiddling around with their cell phone or PDA during an event, they view it as a sign of pompousness. Many people, even CEOs, have fallen into the habit of utilizing these tools anytime, anywhere. If you find you have become one of them, make it a priority to stop!

Be inclusive, attentive, and interested. At events, there are often a few small, tight-knit clusters of people scattered around the room, each one looking more intimidating and impenetrable than the next, similar to your high school lunchroom. Strive to give off the exact opposite vibe. Be inclusive and welcoming to people as they join your conversations. After all, networking is, by definition, an inclusive activity and events are a perfect place to expand your circle of contacts.

There are also people who constantly scan the room, looking to see who else is there that they should be mingling with. Focus on the person you're talking to and be fully engaged; you'll both get more benefit from the interaction this way.

Don't monopolize conversations. It's easy to dominate discussions without even knowing you're doing it. If you realize you have been talking for an uncomfortable length of time, and wish to divert the focus to someone else, try asking others some open-ended questions. You can also use this method to restart a conversation that has stalled awkwardly, or that has merely settled into a natural lull. Try to use people's names when you ask them these questions to emphasize your interest. For example:

1. So, Mary, how are you connected to (name of organization hosting event)?

2. What exactly does your company do, Belinda?

3. What do you do, Roy?

4. Charlie, what are the biggest challenges your industry/company is facing?

RSVP, arrive on time, and leave early only with great discretion. RSVPs are critical for the event's organizers to be able to plan for the appropriate amount of space, food, nametags, and other event resources. If an event does not specifically allow for at-door registration, it will reflect badly on you if you show up anyway. Conversely, it looks bad if you RSVP and then no-show. This is especially true for free events with attendance limits. It all comes down to respect for the event's host.

Arriving on time is the most professional thing to do. You can arrive a *little* early, but you don't want to be in the organizers' way. If you arrive late, you will attract unwanted attention. If you must leave an event before it's concluded, do so discreetly at an appropriate time, such as during a break, or when the wait staff is clearing dishes. If you know ahead of time that you will have to leave a seated event early, try to sit close to the exit. Also, if you're at an event where you're seated around a table, bid your tablemates farewell as you depart. You should let them know why you are leaving early to avoid giving them the impression that they have driven you away.

Take Aways

Join organizations and attend events to build, expand, and maintain your network.

Choose organizations that will be the best use of your time.

Use proper event etiquette so you come across professional, polished, and personable.

7

MENTORS, PEER GROUPS, & ADVISORY BOARDS: SEEKING COUNSEL ACROSS THE GENERATIONS

The road to building a career is a bumpy one; it's long, winding, and full of potholes. And since everyone must find their own way, there's no map or GPS device to consult. Occasionally you come across a fork in the road. That's when it's helpful to have extraordinary people to whom you can turn for guidance. These people can be invaluable to your long-term success, and can help you avoid many of the potholes along the way.

Your mentors, peers, and advisors will be from one of the four generations working side by side in today's workforce.

- Matures (born 1901-1945)
- Baby Boomers (born 1946-1964)
- Generation X (born 1965-1978)
- Millennials or Generation Y (born 1979-1988)

To be a successful networker, it's important to not only understand how each generation communicates, but how people from each generation expect to be communicated with. If you want someone's advice, you're going to have to approach them according to their communication style, *not yours*. In this chapter, we'll explain how to find, approach, and network with successful professionals from the different generations.

What exactly is a mentor?

A mentor is a trusted advisor who can help advance your career by offering counsel, support, and even introductions to other successful professionals. Anyone with more experience than you can be your mentor, but the most helpful mentors have usually been working several decades longer than you.

The relationship can be a formal one where you refer to them as your mentor and meet on a regularly scheduled basis. Or, you might simply call them whenever you have a specific question or problem. This can be especially helpful if you are dealing with office politics or personal development topics.

Alternatively, the relationship might be so informal that neither of you even realizes you have a mentor-mentee relationship. If there is someone in your life to whom you regularly turn to for career advice, you may already have a mentor. If so, be sure to thank this person for their guidance. Someone who has spent their time and taken a visible interest in assisting you along the path of your career is not someone you want to take for granted.

A mentor can be someone who works at the same company you do. In fact, some companies have formal mentoring programs. Law firms, for example, often assign senior attorneys to work with specific younger lawyers. They teach them how to do their research, introduce them to key people inside the firm, and help them chart their path toward partnership. Of course, a mentor doesn't have to be someone inside your company. (Later in the chapter we'll explain why it's actually beneficial to seek mentors *outside* your company). As long as your mentor is a more experienced professional who will take an interest in your career and offer helpful advice along the way, he or she could be from an entirely different industry.

Anne Says

At one point in my career I was asked to create a strategic marketing plan and present it to my company's C-level executives. While confident in my plan, I was afraid the senior executives would never get a chance to see it because my manager was annoyed that the CEO had asked me to prepare the plan instead of her. I didn't want to slight my manager, but I really wanted the opportunity to present to the senior staff. Not knowing how to handle this, I phoned my mentor.

I met Lois at the Kellogg School of Management at Northwestern University. Lois is an international entrepreneur who always has great stories and advice. Over time, we developed an informal mentoring relationship.

Lois suggested that I request a meeting with my boss to review my marketing plan. She told me to bring Post-it notes, highlighters, and an extra copy of the report with me. Then she explained that I was going to have to let go of the notion that this plan was going to be written just by me. In order to get the marketing plan approved by my boss, who felt slighted by the CEO, I was going to have to ask her to collaborate on the plan with me. Lois was spot on. My boss was thrilled I had asked for her assistance and we ended up having a lot of fun working on the presentation together.

No matter where you find your mentor, having a good one can help you reach your career goals faster because your mentor will help you make better decisions when you come up against unexpected roadblocks. Ultimately, a good mentor is someone that has been there before and, because they have already faced and conquered their own workplace obstacles, he or she looks upon your problems as minor pitfalls.

Finding a mentor

So where do you find this person? Before we discuss a rather formulaic (though useful) process, let's talk about what a mentor *is not*. A mentor is not:

- Someone that you call up to vent all of your career frustrations to.

- There to solve all of your personal problems that are contributing to your lack of concentration at work.

- Responsible for finding you a job.

Most importantly, a successful mentor-mentee relationship cannot be forced. Ever. That's why most formal mentorship programs ultimately fail. You cannot simply call up a successful person and ask them to be your mentor if they have no idea who you are. You have to build a rapport with the person you wish to mentor you. A true mentor is someone who will be in your life for a long time, and who will enjoy watching you grow up in your industry. That type of relationship does not spontaneously bloom into being; it takes time.

To find a mentor, you must first know what type of person is likely to be a good match for you in a mentoring capacity. You'll be more likely to recognize someone who is a match for you if you spend some time brainstorming about the characteristics that your ideal mentor will have. Consider:

1. What type of specific business or industry experience do they have?

2. Does age matter to you?

3. Does their gender matter?

4. What do you really expect them to provide for you?

5. Do you care if your mentor lives in a different state, or country?

Next, make a list of people who you feel meet these ideal requirements. If you're drawing a blank, ask people in your network for suggestions. The last thing you have to do is ask. Unfortunately, it's this last part that's the tricky part!

"Will **you** be my mentor?"

You really want to learn from someone who has "been there, seen it, done that." Most often, for Gen Y, this means finding a mentor from the Baby Boomer generation. As the predominant occupants of the top jobs in corporate America, Baby Boomers possess perhaps the most valuable mentoring advice for a young professional, but they tend to be the most difficult to recruit as mentors. And it's not because they don't want to help the next generation in the workplace, but because they have the least amount of time. Working Boomers already have daily schedules that are bursting at the seams. Still raising children, putting older children through college, and caring for elderly parents, it's hard for Baby Boomers to justify taking on any more responsibilities.

This is not to discourage you from asking a Baby Boomer to be your mentor, but rather to emphasize the importance of *how* and *where* you make your request. Cam Marston is one of the nation's leading experts on generations in the workplace, and author of *Motivating the "What's in it for me?" Workforce: Manage Across the Generational Divide and Increase Profits*. He suggests that you will have more luck convincing someone from the Baby Boomer generation to take on a mentoring role if you arrive "hat in hand" with a deferential attitude when you make the request rather than showing up saying, "here's what I need." According to Marston, you want to avoid the hard sale when connecting with Baby Boomers and even members of Gen X.

He also says that email is *not* the way to begin this type of relationship with a Baby Boomer because it's too impersonal. "You have to follow the rules of the people you wish to connect with and know how they want to be approached—and Baby Boomers prefer an eyeball-to-eyeball approach," he says.

That's not to say you can't make an introduction over email. In today's hyper-cyber world it's likely that you'll find an excellent mentor candidate two degrees away on *LinkedIn*. In this case, Marston advises drafting an email that begins with, "we've never met before." This is a sales technique that has helped many a sales professional woo a new lead or client over email. It works because it disarms the person receiving your message. It drains the interaction of tension and indicates that, as Marston puts it, "you're not trying to cash in any chips with anyone." Using this technique, the introduction section of your email might look something like this:

"You and I have never met before. We have a mutual friend in Mr. Smith and it is through him that I discovered you on *LinkedIn*. I am sending this email to find out if you'd be willing to meet me for a 30-minute informational interview, at a location of your choosing, so that I can ask you about how to most effectively approach a career in the hospitality industry."

We don't advocate making the mentor request in this initial email. That's because in-person one-on-one meetings are the most appropriate place to ask someone to be your mentor. Keep in mind that while networking events are a great place to *meet* a potential mentor, they are not the best place to *propose* a mentoring relationship. You don't want to come on too strong, too fast. It's a major turn-off to Baby Boomers who like to be approached in a more traditional way. If you do meet someone during a networking event who you believe would make a fantastic mentor, you can plant the seed, but definitely refrain from making an outright request.

You could say something like:

> "*I have really enjoyed talking to you this evening and it's clear I could learn a tremendous amount from you about broadcasting. What can I do to work myself into your calendar?*"

The key is to be humble, and to express gratitude for any time the individual would be willing to spend with you. If, at the follow-up meeting, you feel there is a mutual connection, then you may ask the person to be your mentor. Even at that point, however, you want to avoid putting the individual on the spot. Instead of phrasing your request as a yes or no question, you might say:

> *"I wonder if you would give some thought to allowing me to become your mentee? I'd be curious to know what you would expect on my part and what type of commitment you would need from me to make this worth your while. Why don't you think about it some? I'll follow up with you next week if that's agreeable to you."*

The worst they can say is no. Again, most often the reason someone must decline a request to enter a mentoring relationship is due to time constraints. No one wants to commit to something they realize they may not have the time to do properly. It's rarely personal, and should not be interpreted as a sign that they don't think you have potential.

If someone says no to you, thank him or her for their honesty and move on. It is appropriate, however, to ask if you could send them updates about how you're progressing in your career. This is a great way to stay on someone's radar and potentially develop a networking relationship down the road. Keep in mind that these updates should be infrequent, brief, and personalized.

I've been fortunate to have mentors who believed in me before I even believed in myself. Early in my career I worked for a woman named Maureen in the media department at Elizabeth Arden Cosmetics. When Maureen noticed that I was outgrowing my position at Arden, she encouraged me to explore magazine advertising sales. Maureen helped me rehearse my presentations in preparation for my interview. She offered constructive criticism and positive feedback until I landed a job at Town and Country magazine and then she became my client as well as friend. Sometime after that I co-founded MyWorkButterfly.com, a social networking site for return to work and working moms. Maureen was one of our first members and stood proudly as we launched the brand at the home of Malaak and Chris Rock in January 2009. Now that's taking mentorship to new heights!

Bradi Nathan
Co-Founder
MyWorkButterfly.com

What exactly is an advisory board?

As you attend events and expand your network, chances are you'll meet several people who you'd like to ask to be your mentor. You might begin to wonder how you can possibly narrow it down to just one. Fortunately you don't have to. In fact, it's better to have multiple advisors as opposed to just one mentor. This way you can receive advice from several different perspectives.

This is one reason why it's helpful to have a mentor within your company, as well as a mentor who works elsewhere. For example, a mentor within your company will have certain biases (whether consciously or subconsciously) toward people you work with. On the other hand, a mentor who works outside of your company may have a more objective opinion about how you should handle an issue with one of your co-workers.

Sometimes it's appropriate for your mentors to know about each other, and other times it isn't. Use your best judgment in determining how open you are about the mentoring relationships you have. It is critical that you maintain confidences at all times however, especially if you have mentors from two competing companies or firms.

Where to find advisors

To find potential advisory board candidates you can follow the same three-step process that we described for finding a mentor. However, if you know, or are acquainted with, someone from the Mature generation who still occupies a prestigious position within his or her company, look no further. Though not likely to make an appearance at the next company happy hour, if you invest the time to connect with a Mature, and they take you on as a mentee, you will be very fortunate indeed. Matures have survived several downturns in the economy, and they've watched corporate fads come and go. They've seen it all, but unless they transfer their knowledge to someone who wants to learn, all that wisdom and experience will be lost.

When requesting a mentor-mentee relationship with a Mature, you should show the same deference you would to a Baby Boomer... *and then some.* Instead of asking a Mature to mentor you, you might first ask if you can job shadow them. This opens the door for a potential relationship, but doesn't put them in the position of having to commit right away. Often Matures have so much knowledge stored away in their heads that they themselves don't even realize how much they know. Developing a long-term relationship will prove more beneficial than a brief 30-minute informational interview, because as a mentee or friend, you'll be able to tap into that knowledge for years to come—long after they've retired.

What exactly is a Peer Group?

A peer group is made up of people at similar places in their careers that act as a personal advisory board to each other. For graduates looking for their first real job, or for young professionals moving into new career territory, having others to turn to for advice and support makes the journey less frustrating and lonely. Many entrepreneurs use this model of meeting with other entrepreneurs to share best practices. Ideally, a peer group becomes an open and safe environment to discuss career goals, compare job search strategies, make new connections, and test business ideas.

Thom Says

In my twenties I started to notice that some people were pulling ahead of others, career-wise. I wanted to get ahead, but was unsure exactly how to do it. Two friends and I discussed forming a group with whom we could, over time, develop a trusting and mutually beneficial relationship. There were seven of us: four men and three women, all from non-competitive industries. We were either in sales or were small business owners. We agreed to meet twice a month, once for breakfast, the other for happy hour, with a one-year commitment. At the end of that year we would evaluate the group's effectiveness.

Our first few gatherings were spent getting to know each other and developing ground rules. With seven energetic individuals, it took little time for us to become fast friends. Over the next year we took turns sharing our ambitions and career pitfalls. Others in the group could chime in and make recommendations, and/or make introductions to others in our networks that could be of assistance. In time we came to see each other as shoulders to lean on, sounding boards, and advisors. The group was made up of a diverse group of professionals with different perspectives and unique views of business interactions. While each person had extensive local contacts, those contacts were not from the same industries.

After a year, we all agreed that the group was instrumental in our career growth. Three members had successfully surpassed sales quotas, one made partner in her firm, another started his own business, and another found a better job. During the second year three members dropped out because of life changes. But the four remaining members kept the group going. Many things happened in our lives, personally and professionally; we shared successes and failures. Yet each of us will tell you that we were better off because of the group than we ever would have been on our own. While we are no longer a formal peer group, we are still friends, and I still turn to them for advice.

Organizing your own Peer Group

When starting your own peer group, it's important to include people other than just your friends. It's fine to start with one or two people you already know and build out from there. While it's not crucial to keep the group's existence a secret, it's advisable because it prevents others from asking to join and allows you to be more selective about whom you include. You'll also want to decide how large or small you want your peer group to be.

Once the group has gotten underway, it gets more difficult to add people because having to sit through lengthy introductions at every meeting becomes cumbersome. A good number for a peer group later in your career is between five and eight. However, when you're starting out, the more people you can include the better; for recent grads this can be between eight and twelve people. This allows for some attrition, and the group remains small enough where everyone can really get to know each other.

Set ground rules early. If someone's work schedule is irregular and does not allow them to make most meetings, decide if that's someone you want to keep in the group. In order to get the most benefit out of the group, it may be better to find someone else. Use your best judgment based on the people involved, your relationship with them, and how much benefit you think they can provide to the group.

Confidentiality is a must. Discuss this at your first meeting and get everyone to agree to the group's rules and meeting structure. For example, you want to be sure that everyone gets a chance to talk about themselves and the issues they are facing at the meetings. For the group to succeed, everyone must make attending and participating a priority. Keep in mind that even with a successful group of people who develop close relationships, the group will eventually play itself out. And that's okay—by that time it will have already served its purpose of providing new networking opportunities for everyone.

Avoid Generation Gaffes

Mentors and peers do not serve the same purpose as your mother; they will not hold your hand and promise to make all your troubles go away. Furthermore, it is not their responsibility to anticipate when you're about to step in it, or provide therapeutic venting sessions when you make bad decisions. It takes more than just hanging the title of mentor or peer group member around someone's neck to make the relationship flourish. You have to be accountable to the advice that your mentors and peers are giving you.

While no one appreciates having their advice ignored, this is especially true for Baby Boomers or Matures. If someone from these generations agrees to mentor you, they expect you to follow their advice, or to at least report back to them with an explanation as to why you chose not to. Matures and Baby Boomers view you as a waste of time when you don't make an effort to implement their advice.

Something else to consider is how you process the advice and knowledge that your mentor shares with you. Baby Boomers, Matures, and even Gen X, who did not grow up in the hyper-connected digital universe, will not appreciate seeing your conversations blogged about or tweeted. If you have an especially high-profile mentor, do not take your Flip to lunch and assume they want to be featured on your *Facebook* page. Assume that everything your mentor shares with you is confidential.

By embracing generational diversity, and harnessing the wisdom that each group has to offer, you will expand your network more quickly and create a much more powerful network. In addition, if you are in a very exclusive career field, or have achieved a high level of success early on, be on the lookout for opportunities to become a mentor yourself. Giving of yourself is very rewarding. It can also benefit you directly because as your mentee advances in his or her career and expands their own network, they will be in a position to return the favor and assist you.

Take Aways

A mentor has already achieved what you wish to achieve and is committed to helping you.

A peer group is your personal career advisory board.

Having several mentors allows you to receive advice from several different points of view.

8

THE WIRING:

PLUGGING IN TO SOCIAL

NETWORKS

Most new graduates have grown up on the Internet. The power of online social networking as a communications tool is pervasive in how you live your life. Though social networks make it possible to connect with people who would otherwise be out of reach or simply unknown to us, a social network is not an open invitation to come in the back door and sit down at the kitchen table; you're still expected to ring the doorbell. To reap the rewards of social networks you must approach them using the same steps you do when you're networking offline. After all, at its core, a social network is nothing other than one more place to meet like-minded people.

Which Social Networks Should I Join?

It's hard to answer this question adequately without knowing what your career goals are. However, the professional benefits of belonging to one or more online networking sites can be numerous *if* you follow three simple guidelines.

1. First, the membership of a social networking site must include the demographics of those with whom you wish to connect. For example, if you are pursuing a career in finance, *MySpace* is probably not the best use of your time since it has become a launching pad for aspiring musicians. You would be better off creating a profile on *LinkedIn* and participating in the *LinkedIn* groups related to

finance, where you'll be more likely to meet finance professionals.

2. Second, it's not enough to just join the sites. You need to invest the time to understand the protocol and proper "netiquette"—Internet etiquette—of how to interact with the other members of that particular site. If you're not all speaking the same language, a meaningful conversation is impossible as each social networking site has its own language.

On *Twitter*, for example, you cannot publish anything longer than 140 characters. Therefore, it's vital to know the secret to communicating in a way that's interesting and brief in order to be effective. You need to know how to utilize short URL aliases, abbreviations commonly used in text messaging, hash tags, and a variety of other methods used in the Twitterverse. Someone who has never spent time on *Twitter*, and doesn't take the time to learn these methods, will find networking on that site disorienting and a waste of time.

Furthermore, if you use the brief *Twitter*-style communication technique in communities such as *LinkedIn* groups, you'll be perceived as unprofessional and inarticulate.

3. Finally, set realistic expectations and goals. You will be more satisfied with the results of your networking efforts online if you know what you hope to get out

of it and have an idea of what to expect going in. It's possible that a prospective employer might discover you on *Twitter* or *Facebook*, but it's not likely. There is, however, a better than average chance of your connecting with someone on a social networking site who knows of a company that would be a good fit for you. Never expect your online profile to magically fast forward you to the job of your dreams. You must still take the steps to establish relationships if you want people to help you.

Assuming you follow these guidelines, the benefits of social networking will be many and well worth your efforts.

"With the explosion of social media technologies, students have an incredible opportunity to build a powerful and visible online brand and use it to connect to hiring managers like never before. With hard work, dedication and focus, students can command their career and control their futures one click at a time."

Dan Schawbel, author of Me 2.0
and owner of StudentBranding.com

The Benefits of Social Networking

Many professionals join social networking sites to stay visible. Others belong because they want to meet influential people who can help advance their careers. No matter what your primary motivation is for plugging into a social network, one thing is for certain: if you focus your efforts on being a positive, active contributor to the network, the benefits of membership will eventually outnumber the reasons you joined. Here are four benefits that social networks offer specifically for college graduates.

1. Research

Social networking sites are excellent resources for researching practically anything related to your career. Here are a few examples:

Graduate Degrees. Perhaps you've decided to go back to school for an advanced degree. You've looked into a few graduate programs, but don't know how to decide which one will give you the most bang for your buck. One solution is to search social networking sites for user profiles of alumni who have attended the programs you want to enroll in. Find out what types of jobs they have now. Knowing how successful others have been with similar credentials is one way to gauge whether a particular degree or program will be beneficial for you. You can also search for students currently enrolled in a program and compare their background to yours. Finally, you will also get a general sense of how respected that program is in your industry by determining which companies have hired its alumni.

Career Paths. A question many recent graduates have is: What type of job does my degree qualify me for? Social networking sites can help you answer this question in a few ways. You can do the same type of search as if you were researching graduate degrees by viewing user profiles, or you can take advantage of the interactive nature of social networking sites and simply ask fellow members for advice. Many experienced professionals on these sites are happy to offer career advice and suggestions to recent graduates. Studying the progression of job titles in member profiles will also give you an idea of different career paths you could follow.

Employers. When *you apply* for a job through a job board, or through your college career center, you know which company you have submitted your résumés to. That is not always the case when a company *contacts you* online. New graduates need to be extra diligent about researching employment opportunities with companies they have never heard of before. Researching what the people who work for that company have to say about it is one way to find out what it would really be like to work there. Remember, it's easy for a company to upload a flashy website and say a lot of great stuff about their mission and values, but it's a lot more credible when employees and customers are saying great things about the company.

People. Social networking sites are by far the most accessible resource for learning more about the people you wish to network with: colleagues, potential mentors, manages, professors, friends of friends, and the list goes on. Remember that you are being queried as well.

Colleen was struggling with whether or not to return to school for a master's degree. As she began to research programs online, she realized she not only had to select a school, but she had to choose a specialization, too. When she started meeting with admissions counselors from each school they all said practically the same things. They claimed that their curriculum was highly respected by employers and that over 90% of graduates found jobs. Colleen was more confused than ever.

It wasn't until Colleen joined *LinkedIn* and started querying its members that she felt confident making a decision. The people she met on *LinkedIn* were current and former students of the various degree programs and were able to give Colleen firsthand accounts of their experiences in each program. She also corresponded with professors and employers who had hired alumni with the specialization that she ultimately chose.

2. Visibility

Another benefit of social networks is that your profile is visible at all times, even when you're sleeping. Not only can you research other profiles and contact people, but you can list what kinds of networking opportunities you're interested in, and invite people to approach you.

Your public profile on these websites makes it easy for other people to locate you. Whether you are searching for a job, or merely hoping to expand your network, it's essential that you make it as effortless as possible for people to locate you. One way to do that is to make sure your profile is updated frequently and looks professional. Use a professional headshot. Double- and triple-check that your contact information is correct. You don't want to make it hard to find you when you're eager to be found.

It used to be that professional headshots were expensive and difficult to utilize. Today there are photographers who take your photos for a reasonable price and give you the digital files for your extended usage. The best way to find a good photographer is to ask people in your network. Look at your friends' profiles on **LinkedIn** or **Facebook**. When you see local contacts with a great picture, ask them who took the shots. Also, remember to update your photos every few years as you want to look current.

Recruiters also use these tools to find candidates for job openings. Always call recruiters back, even if you are not interested in the particular opportunity. Recruiters can be amazing contacts for you. Just because you are not interested in an opportunity today doesn't mean you won't be in a few years. Be excited when you return the call and listen to what they have to say. If you are not interested, let them know, but always find out the complete details of the job they are trying to fill. You might know someone who would be an ideal fit, and both the recruiter and the potential candidate would benefit from an introduction. And remember, be sure to return their phone call if you don't want to be overlooked in the future.

3. Organization

People change jobs so often that it's easy to lose touch when email addresses and phone numbers change. Social networking sites make it easy to keep track of the people in your network because you're not responsible for keeping everyone's information up to date, they are. Some sites even offer functionality that alerts you when your contacts update their profiles.

In addition, these sites make it simple for you to see whom your contacts are connected with. Sometimes these connections are kept private, but often they are viewable. By regularly reviewing the lists of whom your friends are connected to, you can identify business professionals you'd like to meet. Often you will be surprised to discover that the person who can make a career-changing introduction is someone you regularly speak with.

4. Global Outreach

Online networking is an incredibly valuable tool when you do business outside your immediate geography, or when you're looking to relocate to a different geography. Look for people you want to know in the city you will be going to and use your online social network to gain advance introductions to key individuals in that city. Before arriving, schedule coffee, lunch, and dinners with new people so that you can build your network on a national or even international basis. By planning ahead, you can keep your calendar full while traveling and maximize your networking opportunities.

Thom Says

My work as a professional speaker involves constant travel so once a month I scan through my contacts on *LinkedIn* or *Facebook*. I review their contacts to see if there is anyone I should meet in the cities I will be traveling to. I select one or two people that I want to know and then I call my contacts to strategize the best way to obtain an introduction. I never blindly reach out to someone and drop the name of a mutual friend or ask for an email introduction, as I realize that everyone is different, and talking with the mutual friend in advance helps to create a more meaningful and appropriate connection.

Netiquette

People have varying levels of comfort when it comes to sharing personal information online. While some people value their online network and work hard to nurture it, others see it as a nuisance. Since you can't read body language, or hear someone's tone of voice when communicating online, it's easy to be misunderstood or even to offend someone without meaning to. Making a good first impression online is even more critical than in person because you may never get a second chance to redeem yourself if you're blocked or all your messages are sent directly to the junk folder.

To help you make the best possible impression on social networks, here are a few rules to keep in mind.

Clumsy **vs.** Classy Introductions

Just because someone has a profile on one of these sites does not mean they welcome everyone on the planet to contact them. Just as when you meet someone face-to-face, you need to follow the steps to properly begin a conversation online. Do not assume that just because you stumbled upon them online, you can send a casual note that reads like a text message. Craft clear, concise introductory messages that leave little room for misinterpretation, and that merely express your reasons for wanting to develop the relationship further.

In addition, when someone accepts your invitation to join a social network, that is not permission to send your life story in an email with your résumés attached. The beginning of a relationship is not the right time to ask someone you barely know to do you a favor. It is, however, a great time to look for ways to help them out.

Presenting the Right Image

Social networking actually presents a rather gigantic conundrum for recent graduates who have grown up in the digital age. Since it's highly likely that you already belong to online communities such as *Flickr, Twitter, Facebook, LinkedIn, MySpace, Friendster, Digg, Technorati, Squidoo,* it's also likely that most of your entries, photos, and interactions on any of these sites occurred when you were a teenager and college student, not a job seeker. Therefore, the all-too-readily-available and easily searchable information about you online may be several years old, yet still off-putting to potential employers.

Here's the problem. Even if an employer has a policy that states they don't care what their employees do online, a client of that company might. Or, a competitor looking to recruit new talent might. Keep in mind that anything you say on a blog or in a social networking forum can be found by someone who you may need to impress someday. It's better that you take down anything online that could embarrass you or your current or future employer. Don't make the mistake of thinking that people make a distinction between the professional you and the real you. There is no such distinction.

Quantity **vs.** Quality

A social network is not a shortcut to building a large, influential network. Having thousands of contacts, friends, or followers means very little if you have not developed a true relationship with those people. In fact, savvy people view link collecting as an amateur networking tactic. Linking to strangers just to have big numbers will make your online network a fraud.

People who do not enjoy networking view these sites as the magic solution to building relationships. They look at their number of contacts and fail to differentiate between the quantity of links and the quality of their network. It is very difficult to get to know someone simply by reading his or her profile. Social networks are not a something-for-nothing proposition, meaning even if you're linked to someone online, if you can't pick up the phone and call that person (because you're not sure they'd take your call), then that person is *not* part of your network.

There are people on *LinkedIn* called "LIONS" (*LinkedIn* Open Networkers) who want to link to as many people as they can, even when they do not know the other people directly. Many of these people brag about their huge networks. However, this is akin to having a copy of the Los Angeles County Phone Book and claiming you can reach 10 million people (after all, you have their phone numbers).

Ultimately, social networking can be a wonderful supplement to your networking efforts offline, but that's really all it is—an enhancement.

How Much Time Should I Spend Networking Online?

Members in online communities are not prescreened. Therefore you have no way of knowing exactly whom you're going to meet or what their motivations are. Spend too much time networking with the wrong people and social networking becomes more of a time suck than anything else. To meet these people who may change the trajectory of your career as quickly as possible you need to be strategic about how you utilize your time on these networks.

To start, jot down a few goals. These goals need to spell out exactly what you hope to gain from each network that you belong to. Once you've done that, break down how many hours per week you'll need to spend online to reach your goal. If the number of hours seems realistic for you, then you're mapping out a good strategy. No matter what your goals are, you must spend enough time on social networks to do the following:

> **Keep your profile updated.** Almost every social network requires you to create an online profile. Some people do this the day they sign up and then never bother with it again. We've all seen the profiles with major gaps in the About You section, or with no pho-

tograph. This is at best a half-hearted attempt to be involved in an online community. This is like a person who shows up to an event, but sits in the back and doesn't say anything to anyone. To have power in your network, you have to be engaged (online or in person). If you aren't, why bother?

If you're not quite sure what to include in your profile, or how to say it, research the profiles of successful members of the network before completing and publishing your own. This will help ensure you're speaking the same language as everyone else.

Once your profile is active, keep it updated. People are more likely to reach out to someone who keeps their information current.

Be an active part of the community. Get engaged. Make contributions to the discussions, and strive to be a real part of the group. There's no point in joining a network if you don't plan to participate in it. At first it may seem a little awkward, or as if no one is paying attention, but after people have enough time to get a sense of who you are, you'll see your inbox filling up with introductions from people you'll be glad to know.

Achieve credibility. As you participate in social networks, remember that you are no longer a student. You must project a professional image now or people in your industry will not take you seriously. Ways to damage your credibility include: using SMS slang, misspelling words, posting negative comments, and crafting an online image that is entirely different from the real life version.

Know when to move on. If, after a while, a certain network just isn't providing the results you hoped for, cut your losses and move on.

Take Aways

Embrace online social networking as an important tool to help build your network.

Only join online communities that meet your individual needs.

Manage what information you make available to the public, and make sure it is current and casts you in a professional light.

9

UPS AND DOWNS:
THE REAL LIFE STORIES
OF NETWORKING

If you make networking a priority in your life, chances are good that at some point in your career—simply due to the sheer number of interactions you'll have with other people—you'll have some very funny stories to tell and a misstep or two. The most important thing to remember when this happens is that ultimately, your reaction to a networking blunder is far more significant than the blunder itself.

Most networking blunders are nothing more than innocuous gaffes that occur when you're tired, nervous, distracted, or simply new to networking. In circumstances where people immediately recognize that it's an innocent mistake, they laugh with you and there's no urgent need for damage control. In other situations where people aren't quite as understanding, or if the blunder was rather serious, a swift response on your part is required to show that you understand a mistake was made and that it won't happen again if you can help it.

This chapter is devoted to things that sometimes happen when networking and how to get through them.

When Your Mind and Body Aren't Connecting

Why is it that at exactly the moment we want to impress someone, our brain stops communicating with our body? Jeanette was the arts editor for a regional magazine, and as such, it was part of her job to attend gallery openings and interview the individual gallery directors and artists.

Normally she had no trouble meeting new people, but one morning, at a networking breakfast, her cold medication kicked into overdrive and all of a sudden she felt completely numb. Without warning, she randomly lurched into the buffet table, spilling hot coffee all over a woman she had been introduced to just minutes earlier, the director of a major art museum. Unfortunately for Jeanette, who apologized immediately and profusely, the woman angrily waved her away, clearly annoyed and no longer interested in conversing.

In this situation, Jeanette did a good thing by apologizing immediately. In any inopportune circumstance like this, it's key to remember that the only thing you have control over is your *own* behavior. If someone else's reaction to an innocent mistake is over the top or irrational, you have to let it go: consider it a missed networking opportunity, and move on for your own sanity. In the months and years that followed this incident, Jeanette continued to have a working relationship with this woman, though it was strained.

The fact that the relationship was strained was a result of how the two women *reacted* to the incident, not a direct result of the incident itself. For example, an embarrassing situation could happen to you, but result in an entirely different outcome.

Michelle, a writer, was mingling at a local networking event when she heard a lady calling her name. From far across the room the woman cried, "Michelle honey, you've got toilet paper hanging out your pants." Mortified but coolly, Michelle removed the toilet paper, threw it out and continued to circulate. She shrugged it off and didn't let a few seconds of embarrassment rob her of an opportunity to meet people. Coincidentally, another person at the event had been looking forward to meeting Michelle, but soon after arriving, realized he had no idea what she looked like. The toilet paper hanging out of the back of her pants caught his attention, and because Michelle had enough poise to go on with her evening, they struck up a conversation that turned into a professional opportunity for Michelle down the road.

Note: If you are the one who sees see someone sporting a roll of toilet paper out of the back of their trousers, it would be more discreet to tell them quietly instead of yelling it across the room.

I attended an event in New York that was sponsored by a major radio station. After the event, I stood on line to meet the station's news director to chat with him regarding a client of mine being a guest on one of the programs.

As my turn came, I walked up to shake his hand, tripped and fell directly on him. His response was, "Wow, I love when a beautiful woman falls for me!"

However, this incident actually made following up with him easy. I reminded him in my follow-up email: I'm Debra Dixon. The woman who fell for you at the Networking Breakfast a few days ago. And he followed right up with me and is now a valuable resource in my media database.

Debra Dixon
CEO, Light of Gold PR and Marketing LLC
New York, NY

When You Don't Say *Exactly* What You Mean

Romana owned a company that contracted out security guards to various companies. At a networking event she attended, everyone was asked to give a quick introduction. Normally Romana used a great elevator speech that she had prepared for situations just like this one, but for some reason she decided to follow the pattern that everyone else was using that day, which was, "Hello my name is (so-and-so) and I do (such-and-such)." So when it was her turn, she said, "Hello, my name is Romana Evans and I do security guards." Understandably, the entire room burst into laughter.

Obviously this was an innocent error, and as soon as Romana stopped laughing herself, she reverted to her usual elevator speech, which was well received by the good-humored crowd. Romana's story is a great example of a networking blunder that doesn't require damage control. On the other hand, there are circumstances where misspeaking can have more disastrous consequences.

Juan, a recent college grad, had just begun his job with a large manufacturing company when his manager asked him to attend a two-day conference for packaging professionals. During the evening cocktail party on the first night, he was introduced to Denise, one of the VPs at his company. When they went to shake hands, both of them were holding drinks, and somehow Denise's mixing straw caught her sleeve and the maraschino cherry from her drink landed on Juan's suit. At a break out session the next day, Juan's manager introduced Juan to Denise, not knowing that they had already met. Trying to be witty, Juan said, "We're old friends already. She shared her [garnish] with me last night." (Only, he didn't say garnish!) As soon as the words were out of his mouth he realized what a major blunder he'd made, but it was too late. That was extremely inappropriate and though Denise was cordial about it, Juan never advanced in that company and eventually left.

The take away from this example is that whatever you do when you're networking can have a major impact, good or bad, on your future. When in doubt, be conservative. Don't try to be funny if you don't know the people you're talking to well, or if you don't know how it will go over. *Never* make jokes that can have a sexual or otherwise controversial connotation, as they are almost always inappropriate. In this case, Juan would have been much better off to simply acknowledge that he had met Denise, and then get down to business in the breakout session. His remarks came off as arrogant, sexist, and immature. It also didn't help that he appeared to be hung over as well. Which leads us to...

Drinking and Talking Don't Mix

At networking functions, keep your liquor consumption to a minimum, especially early in your career. It's harder to recover from a disastrous first impression than it is from an unfortunate incident late in a well-established career. In other words, the CEO who has a little too much to drink at the holiday party and slurs through dinner will be forgiven much faster than the entry-level media buying assistant who gets drunk at the same event. If you want to avoid a drinking-related blunder, limit yourself to one beer or glass of wine at all work-related events.

If you do make a fool out yourself because you drink too much in a networking situation, the only thing you can do is to apologize afterwards, and make sure it doesn't happen again. Over time you should be able to regain the trust of your co-workers and managers, but why put yourself in this position in the first place? When it comes to drunken disasters, it is much better to avoid them altogether than to have to repair them.

When You *Do* Forget a Face

Forgetting someone's name or getting two people mixed up at an event are two of the most common networking blunders. For example, Mario attended a large, black-tie networking event where he confused two men wearing similar tuxedos. Upon realizing that he had addressed one of the men by the wrong name several times during the course of ten-minute conversation, he acknowledged the mistake and actually introduced him to the other gentleman.

To avoid forgetting the name of a person you've just met, it helps to focus on some distinguishable personal feature that has nothing to do with clothes. Then, in your mind, repeat the person's name while focusing on that feature. For example, Anne has been told repeated times that the big *brown* freckle in the middle of her nose has helped people remember that her last name is Brown.

If you do forget someone's name, you want to shift the focus of the conversation away from the fact that you've forgotten a name and on to more productive networking topics.

For example, here is what you could say if you see someone that you want to talk to, but you cannot remember his name.

"Hello, I know we met before at the last meeting, but your name is escaping me at the moment. I'm sorry, could you please remind me?"

"Rick."

"Rick, I wanted to talk to you because I remember you said your company had a lot of success with your new social media campaign. Could you tell me more about that?"

Or, let's say someone walks up to you and starts chatting as if you're old friends, only you don't recognize this person at all.

"...and then he told me to get the report on his desk by Monday morning or else! Well, you can imagine how I felt about that! Anyway, it's just not the same now that Andy's our new manager and...."

"I am so sorry to interrupt you, but I am having the worst time remembering how you and I met. Could you remind me so that I can concentrate on what you're saying?"

At this point the person might look at you and realize that they're talking to the wrong person, or they'll remind you and you can say, "Oh my gosh, that's right. I'm having an off day." Then you continue your discussion.

Now, what happens if you forget someone's name and they let you know in a rather rude manner? Consider the following scenario.

James, a high-profile executive at a Fortune 500 company, had just arrived at a networking dinner and was checking his coat when someone called out to him from the bar. He turned around to see a young man that he didn't recognize walking up to him. The man said, "James, good to see you again," then just stood there, expectantly. Not knowing who this was, James simply said, "I'm sorry, but I'm blanking on your name. Could you remind me how we know each other?"

The other man was obviously insulted and said somewhat huffily, "We met two years ago when you spoke at our alumni association event. I'm Kevin Smith."

While James would have been justified in saying something else, he politely said, "Well, it's nice to see you again, Kevin."

The point is, people cannot be expected to remember every single person they meet. Most people understand this and are quite gracious in these circumstances; however, others aren't. If someone is rude to you because you forgot his or her name, don't be impolite, (even if it would be justified), but move on. Chances are, they have an overinflated ego and aren't worth your time anyway.

When You Discover What *Not* to Wear

At networking events, you want to stand out, not stick out. Remember the tuxedos that Jim Carey's and Jeff Daniels' characters wore to a black tie fundraiser in the movie *Dumb and Dumber?* Though they didn't notice that everyone gasped as they walked in, chances are you would! Being in a roomful of strangers is intimidating enough without being embarrassed about what you're wearing. It's hard to come across as confident and engaging when you're feeling self-conscious. That's why it's helpful, when possible, to inquire ahead of time about the dress code with the event organizers, or the person who invited you. You're more likely to make the most of a networking event when you're on the top of your game.

Early in his IT career, Aiden was invited to a golf outing that the accounting firm he worked for was hosting for some of the summer interns. The outing was at a private golf course that most of the partners in the firm belonged to. Most of the party showed up wearing khakis, polo shirts, and baseball caps or visors. Aiden, on the other hand, appeared in jeans and a "Who's Your Daddy?" t-shirt. Of course Aiden was not a golfer and the manager who invited him knew this. However, Aiden could have saved himself from the unkind stares and whispers he endured for the rest of the day had he simply asked someone who golfed what he should wear.

Fortunately, Aiden's bosses were all good-natured about the situation. For his next birthday at the office, instead of the traditional gift certificate, they gave him a golf shirt. By that time Aiden was smart enough to wear it at the next summer golf outing with a new pair of khakis!

Anne Says

If someone calls you cheeky, better that it's because of something you said as opposed to something you wore. After having lunch with a former colleague, he invited me to his office to meet some of his co-workers. While I was dressed appropriately, it wasn't until I returned home that I realized the seat of my pants had torn, making the outfit that had started the day as appropriate, undeniably inappropriate. The pants hadn't caught on anything, they had simply ripped from simple wear and tear; they were quite old, though still fashionable. Since then, I am more diligent about inspecting an outfit before putting it on, and less likely to keep clothes made of certain fabrics for more than a few years. I am still mortified when I envision the expressions that must have crossed the faces of the people I met that day as I left their offices. The email from my former colleague the next day explained that I had made a rather "cheeky impression" on his officemates!

Are my clothes *really* that important?

The best answer we can give you is that *it depends*. For example, if you're Steve Jobs you can wear jeans and a black t-shirt anywhere you go and get away with it. If you're not, you might want to put a little more thought into your wardrobe. Danny is the co-founder of a start-up company that designs men's custom dress shirts. While attending a networking event for entrepreneurs seeking venture capital, he met a young man dressed, as he explained, "in a t-shirt he'd had since high school with a stretched collar and worn jeans. I wasn't impressed." That is until he discovered the same young man had started a venture capital firm that had raised tens of millions of dollars for companies similar to Danny's. Suddenly, his clothes seemed very unimportant.

So, yes, it's true that some successful people could wear a hula skirt with neon swim goggles to a networking event and people would still want to talk to them. But when you're starting your career it's wiser to dress more appropriately so that you won't scare people off. You want to be approachable and invite others to engage with you. When you dress in a way that makes you stick out instead of stand out, you'll find people are less likely to initiate an interaction with you.

Making the most of a bad situation

If you can recover from a networking blunder with grace and poise, most people won't even recall the error you made in the first place. To save a potentially bad situation from turning into a full-blown networking catastrophe, you must mentally measure the situation and rely on your own judgment to guide your next move. Remember that the worst thing you can do is draw more unflattering attention to yourself by carrying on about the networking blunder you've committed. Maintain a sense of humor and keep in mind that it's not the end of the world; we've all been there.

Take Aways

There are ups and downs in networking; and mistakes happen. Chances are if you spend any time networking at all, you will make one too. Don't beat yourself up over it.

The right thing to do if you spill something on someone is to apologize immediately (and offer to pay for their dry cleaning).

When you are face-to-face with someone whose name you have forgotten, be up front about it. It's better to be honest and to move on from there, than to come off as insincere.

10

MAINTENANCE: KEEPING
YOUR NETWORK BUZZING

Critics compare networking to having a second full-time job and claim that "schmoozers" cannot possibly have enough time to do their real jobs. In actuality, the better connected someone is, the easier his or her job becomes. The naysayers are right about one thing however: networking requires a real time commitment.

If you want to build and maintain a professional network strong enough to support you throughout your career, you need to remain visible to your existing network as you continue to build new professional relationships. To do this, you need to stay informed about what the people in your network are doing and reach out to them when they need support, or when they deserve a pat on the back. Your network wants to know you are paying attention. This takes an incredible time commitment, one that most recent graduates are not willing to make. For those few who do, however, the rewards are enough to silence even the most outspoken critics.

"Relationships are the result of effort. Unless you are willing to accept that, you won't create positive ripples or build productive relationships."

—*Steve Harper*
author of The Ripple Effect

Cultivate

If you only have a small network, keeping in touch can be an easy thing. You will run into people, exchange phone calls or emails, and be able to keep the relationship alive with very little planning and effort. However, as your database grows and your clients, prospects, and friends expand into the hundreds, it becomes much harder to just let the process happen. You need to find ways to reach large numbers of people at one time without its becoming too impersonal. Here are a few ways you can reach out to your contacts:

Email Updates

These are a great way to keep a large network up to date about you, your career, and your company. Never hesitate to send an email update to your contacts when you accept a job offer or have another exciting announcement to make. Since mass emails are somewhat impersonal, at least segment your contact list into groups and customize your message for each one. Your groups might include: close friends, clients, potential clients, peers, and fellow members of professional organizations.

Extend Invitations

You can reach out to people by inviting them to events or seminars hosted by your company. These can be large, multi-day events or smaller, more intimate gatherings. You could also invite people to attend events hosted by local networking organizations you belong to, or other professional programs in the community.

Alternatively, if you or a prominent individual at your company has a high-profile speaking engagement, use this as an opportunity to reach out to your network. Think about who would benefit from attending the event and invite them to attend as your guest.

Share Information

For natural networkers, sharing interesting information with their network is second nature. For everyone else it's the perfect excuse to get in touch with someone, and to help maintain your connection with that person. If you come across a rare factoid, or interesting news article that someone in your network would enjoy hearing about, let them know about it. This is a great way to let people know you value your relationship with them.

Acknowledge

Times change. You must stay on top of what is happening in and around your network. People get promoted, change companies, and win awards. Outstanding industry stars, people who volunteer with non-profits, or members of high-profile boards will receive accolades in the press. These are all opportunities for you to continue to build on your relationship with others by acknowledging their accomplishments.

Thom Says

On an American Airlines flight, I read an article about executive coaching in which an acquaintance of mine was quoted. Following my return to the office I sent him an email commenting on some of the more interesting points he had made and mentioned that I still had my copy of the magazine. He responded that, sure enough, he had not yet seen it. You can guess what happened next. It was a great chance to get to know him better that came about all because of a free copy of an airline in-flight magazine.

Support the lows

You also want to be sure to keep up with what is happening in the community economically, because not all news is good news. This includes both business and personal hardships. Companies go out of business and people lose their jobs. In addition to finding ways to offer your support during rough times, you need to keep abreast of what is happening so as not to embarrass yourself in conversation.

Thom Says

Soon after the collapse of Brobeck, Phleger & Harrison, where I had worked for two years, in one of the largest public failures of an international law firm in history, I ran into an acquaintance. After exchanging pleasantries he asked me how things were at Brobeck. It became clear that he had no idea that the firm had dissolved. When I finished bringing him up to date he dug his grave even deeper by saying "funny that it wasn't in the paper." Unfortunately for him, it had been on the front page of all the major news dailies in the country and in most business publications, too.

In addition to business woes, people will have personal crises.

When Thom's infant daughter had to undergo brain surgery, several people in his business network reached out. Their thoughtful support helped make a frightening and stressful experience somewhat easier to handle. In fact, networking ultimately led the Singers from Austin to San Diego to the pediatric neurosurgeon whose new procedure helped their daughter.

Reconnect

We have all lost contact with people we have known, socially or professionally, who have been important to us in some capacity. Take a minute and think of someone you've lost touch with who had a positive impact on you. Whatever happened to them? Are they worth tracking down? Would having them back in your life put a smile on your face? Reconnecting is an excellent way to help build your network. It's easy because you already have a foundation to build upon and, in many situations, there was no particular reason that you drifted apart. It just sort of happened. As should be clear by now, it takes serious effort to grow and maintain fruitful relationships in the business world. If one or both parties do not invest the time, it is easy to lose touch with people.

Exactly how do you make contact with someone you have not spoken to in a long time? Just pick up the phone and place the call. Some people think it's inappropriate to call and say hello after so much time has passed. It's not. Most people are happy to hear from someone they haven't heard from in a while. Who came to mind when you started reading this section? Call them right now.

If you live in the same city, it's possible you'll run into someone you've been thinking of reconnecting with. Take advantage of those chance meetings. Set up a time to get together, arrange a lunch, exchange information on what you're doing now. Basically, invite them back into your life.

Thin the Ranks

On the flipside of reconnecting is purposely removing someone from your network. As in other areas of your life, maintaining a network of business contacts usually means you'll encounter difficult people. In most cases you will just be polite when you cross paths. In some cases, however, you will want to purposely remove them from your network.

Steer clear of anyone who does not show good character and respect for others, or who is exceptionally challenging to deal with. You cannot afford to be affiliated with those who are viewed as not having good ethics. It is your responsibility to make sure that you have a positive give-and-take within your network, and if others are not doing their part, you owe it to yourself to move on.

Tread cautiously when removing people from your circle of contacts. If people feel you are ignoring them or treating them poorly, they will share that information with others. Just let them drift away.

Occasionally, because the drift away method has not worked, you will have to actually tell someone that you do not wish to continue a professional relationship. Similar to ending a romantic relationship, this is not easy. But, if the other person is truly damaging to your network, you may need to tell them that you do not wish to continue the networking relationship. If confrontation is necessary, be as diplomatic and kind as possible. Let them know that you do not feel that you share mutual goals. Most importantly, keep the conversation to yourself. Even in large communities, gossip generally finds its way back to the person who is being discussed. The best policy is to not share your personal feelings about anyone.

While you're busy thinning the ranks of your own network, others are doing the same. How can you be sure that someone won't decide you are not worth their time and effort? One reason people make this decision is if you only make yourself available when you need something. When you only surface to ask for favors or introductions, are you really adding value to someone else's network? When your career is prospering, make it a priority to connect with the key members of your network who have played a role in helping you achieve success. Take the time to do this, and you will stand out as someone who no one wants to lose from their own network.

Take Aways

Cultivate your network by reaching out to the people in your network quarterly at minimum, and by continuing to meet new people.

Acknowledge what is happening in the lives of the individuals in your network and be there to celebrate the highs and support the lows.

Reconnect with those you've lost touch with, but wish you hadn't.

CONCLUSION

People with large, thriving, successful networks understand that other people are a valuable resource. As you begin your career, now's the time to start getting to know others with similar interests and with whom you can cultivate mutually beneficial relationships. Like money in the bank that is both saved for a rainy day and pays interest, your network is important for both today's business and it is an investment in your future.

Career-long employment by the same company is no longer the reality. You probably will work for many organizations in different roles and maybe become an entrepreneur. In either case you are never alone. The people who know, like, and trust you over the decades will continuously bring you new and exciting opportunities. Ignore a chance to network today and you might miss out on a life-changing career opportunity years down the road. Besides, you never know when you might meet your future boss, business partner, or even spouse!

You cannot delegate the creation of your network to someone else, nor can you purchase one. New technologies and social media cannot build your friendships nor replace the personal touch. While the tools we use to communicate have changed over the past decade, the way we are wired as human beings has not changed. To be the first person someone in your network recommends, you must let them know you care about them and their goals. Networking is a two-way street.

Skilled networking leads good professionals to great careers. The most savvy networkers make it look easy, but never forget that in the middle of the word "networking" are the letters w-o-r-k! The results will not happen overnight, and you will not always know when and where the payoff will occur, but we encourage you to embrace the skills we teach in this book and in our seminars. While it might not always be easy to go to business events and then to follow up with the people you meet, over a lifetime you will reap the rewards. Creating a network of professional contacts and turning those into life-long friendships is a never-ending adventure. The best and most successful networkers are the ones who keep at it and have fun along the way!

Best of luck with your career!

Anne and Thom

Anne Brown is a marketing professional with 15 years of experience working for universities, non-profits, start-ups, and large corporations. Prior to starting her own internet marketing company, Aha Media LLC, Anne was the Director of Operations & Senior Web Producer at Sender LLC, a design and digital brand consultancy in Chicago. She is the founder of GradtoGreat.com and co-author of *Grad to Great: Discover the Secrets to Success in Your First Career* (Dalidaze Press, 2007). Anne received her BA from Michigan State University and her MBA from Loyola University in Chicago. She holds the designation of Executive Scholar from the Kellogg School of Management at Northwestern University.

Thom Singer has two decades of marketing and business development experience with firms such as RR Donnelley, Brobeck Phleger & Harrison LLP, Marsh, Inc., and Wells Fargo Bank. He has trained more than 2,000 professionals in the art of building professional contacts that lead to increased business.

Breinigsville, PA USA
21 May 2010
238496BV00003B/4/P

9 781935 547082